Sensitelligent
– a guide to Life –

Ralph Jenkins
Marie Örnesved

www.lightspira.com

Published by LightSpira, Sweden 2012
ISBN 978-91-86613-02-0

Authors: Ralph Jenkins and Marie Örnesved
www.sensitelligent.com

Book design: Recito Förlag / Förlagsservice.se

Love is.

Where love is fear is not.
It sparkles in my eyes like the stars!

My heart is like a glowing fire on a mid-winters night.
Love flows like the energy of spring, bringing new life to all things.

I am like the water in a mountain stream. Lively and full of music.
I feel relaxed and I have a smile on my face.
Nothing stands in my way. I am free to create anything.

I am totally empty and full at the same time.
I am all things and nothing.

I am flowing. Everything blends with me.

I am at one with all there is.

I am.

A PERSONAL CONVERSATION

I do not believe you; this is too incredible to be true. Prove it to me!

There is no proof going into the future. I know that you would like to have proof and guarantees that everything will work out, but there is no proof. Our feelings provide guidance on the way forward. I do not need, and will not be given any proof. The signposts are there along the way because I have a clear and open mind. I do not fear the unknown and I know that what comes my way is right for me.

But how can you trust when you know that this has never worked? The harder I try to make it work, the harder I fall, and that makes me upset, angry and miserable. This is who I am – I am miserable and there is no way that I can ever make it. My friends tell me that I am nice and that I deserve something better, but I suspect that they only tell me that because they pity me. I am a nobody and I might as well stay that way because all efforts only cause me more pain.

You are what you choose to be. I know that you cannot comprehend reality in the same way as I see it. You see it with logical eyes where everything is black and white. Let go of judgement and fear and you will have less pain and worry. You will also invite joy, love and peace. You will never have to fear anything and your life will not have to be controlled. Unexpected and miraculous things will happen and you will be shining!

But that means that the light will be on me. What about all the other people who have more knowledge and experience? Why should I shine and not them?

Now you are again being logical about it. Why would you take the space of someone else? Why can you not shine at the same time as others?

But what would other people think? I do not want to step on anyone's toes. Or maybe that is exactly what I should do. Yes I do want to have more space. I know that I am talented, but I have stepped back because there have always been other people who knew more than me. Maybe I should get on the stage and demand that they listen to me. That's what I will do! Thank you for the advice, I will try that immediately.

Hey, wait a second. I did not say that you should demand more space. I just tried to explain that it is good to always be in your space – so that you stay in your power and then, because you always are true to yourself, you are also true to others. The space that you claim does not cause others to have less space. Do not impose your opinion on them. They are free to do as they want and listen if they choose to.

But I want to be in control now. It is time for them to listen to me. I will demand to be heard.

The only thing that you will achieve with that is that they will be angry with you because you impose your opinions on them. Concentrate on drawing the attention of people who are interested in listening to what you have to say. But please make sure that you believe in what you say, and that you do it from your heart. What is the point in having people listen to you if you cannot say it with your heart?

But I am not free to speak from my heart. There are rules and I do not like them.

But why do you stay if you do not like the rules and your circumstances?

I do not have any alternatives.

There are always alternatives.

That is not true. I do not see any options. When there are no options, how can I choose?

There are always options, but you may not see them from where you are, and you may also fear the consequences of the alternatives. You can decide not to be in the situation that you are in, even if you do not know what the alternative is. It is also about how you choose to see your situation and if you accept it or not. Acceptance is the key to change. Accept the situation. Acknowledge that you do not like the situation you are in. Maybe you are stuck because you are afraid of change? Open up and give yourself permission to receive solutions!

You are right, I am afraid of change. I want to be in control of my life!

That probably means that you miss out on many opportunities that you are being provided with; you choose not to see them as you are too afraid to make the change. What is it that you are afraid of? What is there to fear?

Hey, come on, be real. The world is full of things to be afraid of. Have you never heard of unemployment, starvation, war, kidnapping, car crashes, cancer, death. I can make the list longer if you want!

I get your point, but I choose to see the world from a higher dimension. Your fears are as real as you make them and you also attract what you fear. But have you thought that you also attract other things that you focus your mind on. How about a nice, calm walk in nature? Or a warm meeting with a friend? Or maybe a nice day at work with a lot of inspiration? It is all about what you focus your mind on. And yes, maybe you need to be reminded from time to time about the importance of focusing on the positive and accepting negative experiences in life as opportunities for growth. That is what I am constantly doing, but because you continue to take things personally and because you need proof of everything, then you end up seeing it differently.

I guess so, and I do not understand your way of looking at things.

That is because you are in a different level of consciousness and you and I need to cooperate in a better way. You are needed in order to make things happen in a structured way in the physical world. I am of higher consciousness and that is why I can understand you, and why you have difficulties in understanding me. I would like us to make a journey together so that we can cooperate and coexist in harmony with our energies. That is why I have written down the concept of "fear and control," where I explain everything that creates blocks and holds us back, and "trust and intuition" which will help us concentrate on the positive aspects so that we can hold the right focus. I have even included a reference section for more in-depth study of the relevant and related subjects. I explain why you and I are so different and also what happens when we come together and work in harmony.

8

But if you have written it and you say that I cannot understand things the way you do, how can you expect me to understand this?

It is true that I use the right side of the brain and you use the left, but I have tried really hard to use a language, structure and style that you should be comfortable with. I think you are as interested as I am in having joy, peace and love in life, and the only way to realise these qualities is for us to work together.

Well, I am sceptically interested and I will think about it.

Be Sensitelligent about it instead! To be Sensitelligent is to use both your higher and lower senses in an intelligent way. Let's get started at any page that feels good. Maybe even pick a page randomly. Guidance on the next chapter to read will follow. We might end up reading the whole book or maybe just a few important chapters. It really does not matter. The important thing is to get started!

UNIVERSAL VALUES

WHAT DOES IT MEAN TO BE PRESENT?

Being present is a balanced state of mind that requires you
to think not of the time zones of the past or future, but to be
in the now, this very moment. It is very powerful because
you are living in the now, the "whole of you."

WHAT HAPPENS WITHIN YOU WHEN YOU ARE PRESENT?

All your senses are tuning into what is taking place in your
environment. When you are present you are alert and paying attention to what your task may be. You feel connected
to, and not separated from your work. Whenever you are
present in your workplace you are fully focused on the task
you have. Every moment is a valuable one for you, it is a
unique experience. If not, then you are somewhere else, lost
in the past or in the future. Your job is a valuable asset and
when you are present in your workplace you give it credit
as well as those around you.

WHAT HAPPENS IN YOUR ENVIRONMENT WHEN YOU ARE PRESENT?

Because you are attentive, those around you will feel your presence more strongly than if you were not being present. This is clearly noticeable in your workplace. Your colleagues will also feel that they are being actively involved, which is very positive for all in that environment. When you are present your intuition is working, and that often leads to insights that can highlight something that may need changing or improving in the environment. Then fewer mistakes will be made and you will be more efficient and have greater energy to do things.

HOW DO PEOPLE BEING PRESENT INFLUENCE A WORKING ENVIRONMENT?

People who are fully present influence their working environment in very positive ways as their awareness is fully functional. The affects of this can be far reaching, such as:

- People will feel or know that they are being listened to.

- True dialogue will take place when all are present and this will have the positive effect of reducing mistakes because there are fewer misunderstandings.

- When people around you are present it will encourage you to be the same.

- When people are being present in a working environment it means that they are connected and interested in what is taking place or in what they are doing. This is encouraging for everyone.

- Being present gives a different flow to what you are doing with the effect that you become more efficient.

- Fewer accidents will occur.

WHAT METHODS ARE THERE TO BECOME PRESENT?

- Acceptance is the strongest possible way to be present. It takes you right into the moment. When you accept you are ready to move with a positive force in any direction. Forgiveness is one such direction that can come from acceptance. See chapters "*I accept*" and "*I forgive*".

- It is important to transform your worries as they take you away from being present. Worrying takes your feelings and thoughts into the future as you often worry about something that is about to happen. See chapter "*Worry*."

- Your worries may be related to past negative experiences. This will take you to the past. Transform your negative past experiences. See chapter "*Past experiences*."

- Study your fears and transform them, they have their roots in the past and future. They are illusions that prevent you from being fully present. See chapter "*Fear*."

- Develop your intuition. This will help build your self confidence. The confirmation will come to you in various forms. It can be a feeling that you get or it can be a thought that strikes you. See chapter "*Intuition*."

- "Trust" is an easy word to use, but can be difficult to live by. It is important to develop a greater sense of trust in your Self. This will help remove any resistance you may

have to change because change occurs in every moment.
See chapter *"I trust"* and *"The Self."*

WHAT DOES IT MEAN TO UNDERSTAND YOUR PAIN?

Pain is a symptom of a block that prevents energy flow. In order to understand your pain you first have to know where it is coming from. Is it for example a mental, emotional or physical pain that you are feeling, or several that you feel simultaneously? Pain is often a sign of an imbalance within the physical body that can be created by any of the three categories given here. Mental pain can be caused by an overactive mind, which can be felt, for example, as a headache. Emotional pain can be caused by wanting something strongly which you cannot have (or you deny it to yourself). Physical pain can be stress related, such as back or neck ache. Both the mental and emotional imbalances can be felt physically as they do not have any other place to go. Pain is a messenger that indicates that there is an imbalance. The message is energy that is directed into the body area of imbalance. Much pain is self-created due to ways of thinking or behaving.

WHAT HAPPENS WITHIN YOU WHEN
YOU UNDERSTAND YOUR PAIN?

When you start to understand the reasons behind your pain i.e. the experience that leads to pain and why you attract these experiences, then you will have a clearer picture of yourself and positive change can happen within you. Everything that is going on outside of you is seen by you as a drama, or you may feel a victim of it. Change can only come from within and when you realise this, then the pain will become less. It is important to understand that you may also be carrying another person's pain. This will occur if you take on the responsibility for their pain. Then it can become yours, and the other person may even feel better. This can occur unknowingly on a subconscious level between people. You can help someone in their difficult times, but do not take on responsibility for that person's pain. When you have understood the cause of your pain, then positive steps can be taken to heal and balance that area of the body.

WHAT HAPPENS IN YOUR ENVIRONMENT WHEN
YOU UNDERSTAND YOUR PAIN?

Understanding your pain is the first step and an opportunity for you to take action. As soon as you take positive steps to heal what is causing the pain, then it will help to raise the energy of your environment. People will be positively influenced because you let go of the negativity that is causing the pain.

HOW DO PEOPLE UNDERSTANDING THEIR PAIN
INFLUENCE A WORKING ENVIRONMENT?

When you are pain free then you are able to focus on the work at hand. You can be less aggressive. You can have a more positive outlook towards your working environment because you are not focusing on the pain but on work instead, and the whole environment around you will be more harmonious.

WHAT METHODS ARE THERE TO UNDERSTAND YOUR PAIN?

Understanding pain is about gaining insights into how energies move and affect each of us in a slightly different way. It may help to follow some of these suggestions:

- Be true to the pain and recognise that it is there. We often hide or disguise the fact that we are carrying pain by taking pain killers. Let it be there. Pain can sometimes be reduced just by the fact that you accept it.

- Ask yourself what the pain wants you to look at. Let go of the pain and also the thought, and wait. The answer may come to you in various ways (and it may also take some time) – such as a feeling, something you read or just a hunch that it is likely that your pain is related to a certain feeling or to what is happening in your life. Trust what you feel.

- When you know and understand the *where's* and *why's* of the pain then take positive steps to transform what is needed in order to be pain free. See chapter *"Pain."*

- If possible, try to avoid taking a pill to block out the feelings or the pain. When we take medication, we often run away from the possibility of self-healing. If you are prescribed medication, then follow the doctor's advice.

- Pain often presents us with an opportunity to transform an aspect that may require another approach. Look for its meaning and then pain can disappear as your inner healing process begins.

53

WHAT DOES IT MEAN TO ASK FOR ADVICE AND
GUIDANCE?

If you do not know how to handle a situation that you are
in, you first listen to your inner Self and trust your feelings.
This will guide you to your truth. Your inner feeling may
also tell you to seek advice from another who you feel may
be able to help you. It can also mean that you do not put
yourself before others as you show that you do not have all
the answers. Humility is a powerful and positive quality. If
you can bow to another person – anyone – with a deep sense
of humility, you are showing the other person that you are
being humble. Whenever you are being humble it means
that your Ego is not present. When the Ego is not present
then you will feel free to seek advice from another person
without feeling that you are losing face.

WHAT HAPPENS WITHIN YOU WHEN YOU ASK FOR
ADVICE AND GUIDANCE?

It can be a wise decision to seek counselling from another
person when you feel stuck, or caught up in a situation
where there seems to be no way out. It demonstrates that
you too are not perfect. It allows you to admit to yourself
that you may not have all of the answers, and that a direction can come from another area. It is important that when

you ask for advice that you genuinely would like to receive something back. Otherwise others will see that you are not genuinely interested in their input, and that you are only asking for information not guidance. What you do with the advice or information however is up to you. It may be wise not to create expectations with the person giving you advice. It can easily happen that a person will expect that you will act upon their advice just because you are listening to their point of view.

WHAT HAPPENS IN YOUR ENVIRONMENT WHEN YOU ASK FOR ADVICE AND GUIDANCE?

A trusting environment opens the consciousness in a manner that will encourage others to do the same. If it is not a trusting environment, then it may open up fear and others will feel insecure if, for example, you ask for advice. It is very important that you have good intent when seeking advice – any hidden reason will be subconsciously felt by others.

HOW DO PEOPLE WHO ASK FOR ADVICE AND GUIDANCE INFLUENCE A WORKING ENVIRONMENT?

They encourage problem solving. It can be a creative energy that can encourage comradeship and trust that will empower a greater sense of leadership amongst those who are working in such an environment. It also demonstrates that the Ego is less present to corrupt the working environment.

WHAT METHODS ARE THERE TO ASK FOR ADVICE AND GUIDANCE?

The Ego is the strongest form of energy which uses fear to control you from seeking advice or guidance from another colleague or friend. Here are some tools to use to overcome this:

- Listen to your inner Self and trust the feelings you have. See chapters "*I follow my inner compass*" and "*I trust.*"

- Learn to say no to fear in order to take the next step. See chapter "*Fear.*"

- Learn to say yes, I can! I can ask for advice or help.

- Do not take any form of rejection personally. There can be reasons beyond your own knowledge when someone refuses to help. Continue by asking another person.

- By asking for help, you are empowering others to help. This is trust-building and it gives opportunities for growth!

WHAT DOES IT MEAN TO BE INTUITIVELY CREATIVE?

When you are being intuitive then your consciousness has stepped out of the box – the logical consciousness – and into your higher consciousness. It has moved from the left to the right hemisphere of the brain. You are becoming more spiritually orientated. This means that the Ego and emotions (such as fear) cannot influence your level of thinking as you are in a higher vibration. Your intuitive thought creates greater insight into whatever you are working with. It does so by going beyond the limited views of your logic. For you to be truly intuitive requires a certain amount of self-trust to be established. This requires your thinking to go into the unknown without fear or control issues that are based on self interest.

WHAT HAPPENS WITHIN YOU WHEN YOU ARE INTUITIVE?

You can enter into a new situation without fear, blame, or a sense of failing. Your intuition tells you what is right. Then you will welcome the moment by embracing the experience instead of fearing it. When you are intuitive you are also being innovative. The combined energies of the intuitive and innovative are extremely powerful when embraced because they take you beyond your own structured, logical belief systems. A flash of insight may come to you regarding something that you are working on. You feel strongly about this insight and you know it will help you resolve a problem that the group is working on. But at some point in this process you may doubt the insight and hesitate. Do you then take the next step to act upon that intuitive thought or do you cut it off, block it, or say no to it by telling yourself it is only your imagination at work, it was a crazy idea anyway? Whenever you may be faced with this kind of decision making, please remember that the intuitive knows something that the logical mind does not. You intuit what might be there or is about to happen. This is what your higher intuitive consciousness does. In this process you may face certain fears within yourself, but you know they are not real because they are Ego-based. Your Ego presents this fear in order to stop you from taking that intuitive step into the unknown. Going beyond your fears will allow you to be intuitive. The feelings that rise up within you when you are being intuitive are all positive ones. When your intuition is embraced, then confirmation will follow via a happening or an event that will confirm your original intuitive thought.

WHAT HAPPENS IN YOUR ENVIRONMENT WHEN YOU ARE BEING INTUITIVELY CREATIVE?

The environment will have a stronger feeling of clarity and the feeling will be more positive. This is because the general consciousness within the environment is looking for insight and true meaning of what is taking place within that area. The opposite is to be focused on the negative instead of the positive; asking how to repair the old system to keep it going, rather than transforming it into a new one. Your creativity, when acted upon, will be uplifting to your work colleagues and the environment you are in. Positivity attracts positive energy, this is how energy works, and some would call it the law of attraction.

HOW DO INTUITIVE PEOPLE INFLUENCE A WORKING ENVIRONMENT?

Being intuitive is being innovative, which is like a well of inspiration that feeds your thirst for being creative. When people are willing to take the step into the unknown, then changes will happen in accordance with your intent. If however the energy is blocked by decisions from people resisting change or people that do not have the vision or insight you have, then look for ways to change the system. It could be as simple as saying "no, I want change. Can we look forward instead and not try to fix what is no longer good for us." Move on! Adjust to make changes even if at this moment they are not totally clear. Saying no to the old will open up the opportunity for new experiences to take place. Change is inevitable; it is a fact of life and a universal law. You may be there to make that change, even if at first it is not fully accepted by others. Someone has to, so why not you?

WHAT METHODS ARE THERE TO DEVELOP YOUR INTUITIVE CREATIVITY?

- Learn to trust that first feeling and go with the flow of it. See chapter "*I trust.*"

- Try not to give yourself too much time to think about what the intuitive has given you. It may otherwise become lost due to logical intervention that will prevent the development of the intuitive and innovative idea.

- You activate the intuitive quality of the mind by learning how to quiet the mind. See chapters *"Meditation"* and *"How to meditate."*

- Give yourself permission to be intuitive.

- Go beyond your fear. See chapter *"Fear."*

- It is a positive quality to be different and to think in other ways. To dare to go where others have not yet been makes you a true leader. So trust your Self even if your ideas are different.

WHAT DOES IT MEAN TO DECIDE?

There are fundamental differences between choosing and deciding. All choices are based upon the premise of black or white, right or wrong. This is the Ego's way of choosing; it has preferences and therefore creates separation. Your decision making is however not based upon a boxed view of the world being black or white, right or wrong. It has another view that is holistic in its approach. Whenever you decide – not choose – to do something you are entering your higher consciousness. This means that you are stepping out of the logical-box thinking and into the circle of higher consciousness thinking. From this level of thought you will view the world and all that is happening within it from a holistic point of view. This will give you an oversight of any difficulties you may be facing by viewing them from a compassionate view and not from an Ego point of view. You allow yourself to look beyond the judgement of what is there in order to find solutions that are not based on black and white, or right and wrong. True decision making is unbiased and is for the greater good, the collective oneness.

ALL DECISION MAKING IS BASED UPON TWO
FUNDAMENTAL POINTS:

1. Giving yourself permission to decide. If you do not give yourself permission to decide, then you are likely to end up choosing.

2. Trusting your feelings when you decide, not involving your emotions. Whenever you let your emotions be involved, then you may end up choosing.

WHAT HAPPENS WITHIN YOU WHEN YOU DECIDE?

Whenever you decide – not choose – you are basically stepping into the unknown. This will take courage and insight. When truth is present in your decisions, then your light will empower you. When you express your vision you gain insight. You will prevent confusion by staying strong in your decisions.

WHAT HAPPENS IN YOUR ENVIRONMENT WHEN YOU DECIDE?

With all positive decision making there is only one way for it to move and that is forward. All true decision making carries a positive force that will be felt in any environment in which it is being used. It is often the case that the leaders of a group are left with the final decision, which can have a profound effect on the environment. The outcome of all decisions has the same effect – it creates change. If you create an environment that embraces change rather than an environment that fears change then all decisions will carry a greater degree of positivity. This is of course only true when your decisions have a good intent.

How do people who decide influence a working environment?

Those who decide upon issues with good intent bring a positive force into their workplace. This energy can filter down through the workforce, creating a healthier, positive collective consciousness within the whole group and the environment. This is an opportunity to create a greater sense of trust within the environment.

WHAT METHODS ARE THERE TO DECIDE?

- Integrity must be present in your decision making, i.e. you need to be true to your Self and not influenced by the opinions of other people. See chapters *"I trust"* and *"The Self."*

- Corrupt feelings or emotions must not be connected to your decisions - these can be ulterior motives that are reward- or power based. If any of these are present it will have a negative effect on everyone else in that environment and even further outside. If you have guilt or fear, or if you have an unpleasant feeling about the situation, listen to it. Then ask yourself "what is it that is motivating my decision?" If it is anything negative or Ego-based then it is for the wrong reasons.

- Truth must be the bedrock of all decision making and where the truth is present there can be no fear. So in order to take decisions you first need to make sure that you do not carry a fear related to the decision. See chapter *"Fear."*

- Ask yourself about the decision that you are taking – how does it feel (please do not use your mind here, but your intuition or "stomach feeling"). Do you have a good feeling, a gut feeling?

If yes;
— Is it because you will get a reward, recognition or something that will make you feel better? Then you may want to think again about this – are you being true to your Self – or is it possibly a trap by your Ego?
— If the feeling is positive inside and there are no hidden objectives then you are making a decision.

If no;
— Can the cause of you not feeling good about it be related to fears? Then maybe you need to first try deal with your fear and then think about it again.
— If you do not feel good about it, then it is likely not to harmonise with your truth and you should not take a decision in the direction that you are thinking.

WHAT DOES IT MEAN TO FOLLOW YOUR INNER
COMPASS?

The inner compass speaks through your intuitive qualities, the gut feelings that we often have, but seldom listen too. We all have creative gifts that we would like to share and explore with others. These gifts want to be released and expressed, and we are given countless opportunities to do that but we are often unaware of such opportunities because we can be preoccupied in other areas. You may for example be occupied with your past or future and therefore deny access to your inner compass, which is only available in the present. It is here that we are often lost. The inner compass of course requires you to listen to your Self which can only be accessed when you are present.

WHAT HAPPENS WITHIN YOU WHEN YOU FOLLOW
YOUR INNER COMPASS?

Whenever you are following your inner compass you are being present as you are listening to your inner core. Your inner, core feeling is telling you that this is the right thing to do, or this is the right decision to make. You are being intuitive, often without knowing it. Your inner compass is also about the values of your inner truth, what you hold to be true is your guiding light. The worldly compass points positively

67

to the North, your inner compass points positively towards the truth. This is what your inner core is following: truth. Your truth is empowering you through your integrity. How do you know that you are following your inner compass? You feel good inside, full of energy and alive.

WHAT HAPPENS IN YOUR ENVIRONMENT WHEN YOU FOLLOW YOUR INNER COMPASS?

By following your inner compass your view of life will change. It will change in a positive direction because change occurs from within. You will view your environment from that core place. Then the outer will change automatically because you will become less judgemental and be more accepting instead. Results may not always be visible in the present moment. If you are a leader who has the courage to step into the unknown with your vision when truly listening to the inner compass, you will know that the storm will pass and clarity will return.

HOW DO PEOPLE WHO FOLLOW THEIR INNER COMPASS INFLUENCE A WORKING ENVIRONMENT?

If you can imagine that it is not only you who are following your inner compass, but the greater part of those connected to your work or home environment; how would that feel to you? Most probably very positive! This is because it is a collective consciousness that works together to find solutions. The collective consciousness is not separated by going in different directions. The innovative thinker is following the inner compass. To access the full benefit from the intuitive thinkers then the environment needs to be supportive and open to new ideas. It is for example important that the environment is not controlling everything that they do, and that they are given time and resources to work freely. It is also important that the vision of these individuals corresponds with the greater idea of the company, or there will not be harmony. If harmony is not there then neither is creativity or intuition. When ideas harmonise within the environment and become a team, their energy unites as one consciousness. It brings their inner thoughts into a collective pool that will touch each person individually and collectively at the same time.

WHAT METHODS ARE THERE TO FOLLOW YOUR INNER COMPASS?

- Learn to be present. See chapter "*I am present.*"

- Do not deny your inner feelings by allowing fears to control you or those feelings. See chapters "*Fear*" and "*I take responsibility for my feelings.*"

- Learn to act upon those inner feelings and you will encourage your intuitive qualities to grow and flourish. See chapter "*Intuition.*"

- Your inner compass already knows the way, trust it and follow its direction. See chapter "*I trust.*"

WHAT DOES IT MEAN TO FORGIVE?

True forgiveness comes from the heart and not the mind. You can mentally forgive another person but that is not the kind of forgiveness that is meant here. It has to come from the heart! To forgive another person means that you are in total acceptance of what you feel that person may have done to you, others or themselves that does not correspond to your own core values. It is true that you may have differing values. The core aspect of forgiveness is acceptance, as acceptance brings you and your consciousness right into the present moment from where you are able to forgive. You may not like what has happened and it may be important to say I do not agree. When you truly forgive then you also feel good afterwards. Choosing to accept what happened is important because if you cannot accept, then judgement lies between you and forgiveness. Then the matter is clouded by judgement, which is the pathway of the Ego. Forgiveness is a *"selfless act of compassion."* It is an expression of the heart that has no ties to the Ego; it is an egoless expression of you.

WHAT HAPPENS WITHIN YOU WHEN YOU FORGIVE?

The moment you forgive another person with your heart, you are actually forgiving yourself. This may stop your mind for a moment, but process it a bit more deeply. If you turn the words "I forgive you" around, and say to yourself "I forgive myself," then this is what you are actually doing. You are mirroring yourself by forgiving another person. The mirror is Ego-less; it is your love aspect shining through. Look at it this way: that person could be you, or actually that person is you. Do you seek forgiveness for something? If so, then who is going to forgive you? If you can first forgive yourself then you are taking positive steps forward which will make it possible for you to forgive others. Self-forgiveness transforms guilt and it also transforms doubt about your own ability to bless another person.

WHAT HAPPENS IN YOUR ENVIRONMENT WHEN YOU FORGIVE?

Forgiveness affects any environment in a positive way regardless of where you may be, for example at home or at work. Forgiveness carries no judgement. It is free to express understanding, compassion and love instead of the opposite; which could be anger, judgement and jealousy. By you forgiving another person you are freeing yourself from the negative energy in that area by bringing light and peace into it.

HOW DO PEOPLE WHO FORGIVE INFLUENCE A WORKING ENVIRONMENT?

Forgiveness is of the light, and light is an energy that holds the vibrations of love and truth. When you forgive another person it will affect and touch others with these positive energies. This can only bring a positive charge of energy into the environment that you are in. You are likely to have experienced this on some level, regardless of whether it was you forgiving another person, or you receiving forgiveness.

- Learn that our differences are valuable teachings. See differences as gifts and learn to accept them. See chapter "*I accept.*"

- Learn that the choices of other people are their truth or path in life and learn to accept that.

- Learn to be present. Being present takes you into acceptance and when you are accepting you are also able to truly forgive! See chapter "*I am present.*"

WHAT DOES IT MEAN TO LOVE THE SELF?

Loving your Self means that you accept yourself for who you are. Loving your Self is not egoistic as long as it is not about your identity. The identity is based on outer appearances and positions in life that contain a certain amount of control issues. Love does not control and you can therefore not love your identity. But you can create a dependency to it and then it becomes a need to be someone. This is then your Ego wanting that. Your higher Self is love and is identified by the quality of your heart, compassion and truth. By identifying yourself with these qualities you become egoless. Loving your Self means that you are in complete trust of you. Self love is not homeless because it is within you.

WHAT HAPPENS WITHIN WHEN YOU LOVE YOURSELF?

Whenever you are present in Self love then it is impossible to judge another person. You do not get angry, you accept instead. You hold a greater sense of peace because you are at peace with your Self and others that make up your world. Your sense of purpose in life becomes selfless and you seek to help or serve others with compassion. You hold a greater sense of knowing and you also trust and respect what is happening.

WHAT HAPPENS IN YOUR ENVIRONMENT WHEN YOU LOVE YOURSELF?

It is impossible not to love others when you love your Self. This is felt as a very positive energy wherever you go, be it at home or at work. If you do not love yourself then some of the following negative consequences may arise:

- You overreact because you are emotional.

- You smoke because you are escaping your Self love.

- You drink too much alcohol to comfort yourself as you feel that no one loves you and you do not want to be loved.

HOW DO PEOPLE WHO LOVE THEMSELVES INFLUENCE A WORKING ENVIRONMENT?

This is a mirror of the above points because Self love is a positive force wherever it may be, such as in the working environment. It will not fail to positively influence the consciousness that is present in any working environment. Joy will be present where it previously was not. The environment will also hold a greater sense of peace, and a knowing that all is well.

- If you are angry with another person then you need to look at what you do not accept within yourself or what you are denying yourself. To be angry with others may also be a way of seeking their rejection in order to make them love you or need you. Have a very deep look at what it is that you cannot accept within yourself and also why it is not possible for you to love yourself. See chapter *"Anger."*

- It is important to look at how you treat others, because this is how you treat yourself.

- Transform all the negative energy you may be holding about others and yourself into loving energy.

- Look more deeply at the needs you have. The needs are fulfilling a reward system. To be free to love yourself, transform those needs.

- You can love the Self by being true to yourself. This will help you overcome any difficulties you face in life. Love has the power to transform anything that is negative, Ego-based, fearful, or not true to the meaning of love itself. See chapter *"Love."*

- You are divine and you should build trust in your divinity. To accept your Self means to trust and let your divine energy shine through as "The light of love." See chapters *"I trust"* and *"The Self."*

WHAT DOES IT MEAN TO LOVE OTHERS FOR WHO THEY ARE?

This is deeply connected to acceptance. You can only truly love through acceptance. Whenever you accept something, someone, or a situation you find yourself in, your consciousness, feelings and emotions are present, in the NOW! From there you can let go of any judgement you may have. When you have taken yourself into the now without judgement then you are in the right place to love. The energy of love can only be found and given when you are fully present. Love cannot be found in the emotions, it is in the heart. The energy and vibration of love is not in the lower consciousness, which is why you cannot heal emotions with emotions. Love is a higher consciousness quality, which can only be felt from one moment to the next. In order to love others you have to be present in its vibration for every second, for every minute, for every hour, for every day, for every week, month, year and even a lifetime.

WHAT HAPPENS WITHIN YOU WHEN YOU LOVE OTHERS?

Love is unconditional. Self love gives birth to selfless love. When you accept others for who they are then the Ego is dropped. When the Ego is out of play, then you will have no judgement, fear and no emotional issues. In other words, all your controlling issues are transformed by loving another for who they are. That inner love opens the heart as love is fearless. Love takes you to places where fear cannot reach you as you are carrying the light of love. Whenever love is present, darkness is not.

WHAT HAPPENS IN YOUR ENVIRONMENT WHEN YOU LOVE OTHERS?

Love touches everything because it is unconditional. Where love is, so is peace. A peaceful environment is a loving environment. Love is soul, spirit and body, love is all things. By loving others we share our body, spirit and soul with them in truth. The consciousness of love fills any environment with light.

HOW DO PEOPLE WHO LOVE INFLUENCE A WORKING ENVIRONMENT?

Through your love travels joy, peace, truth and light - they are the messengers of love. Whenever you are present in your love you are also holding these qualities that will touch others in your environment. Greater harmony and joy will be present.

WHAT METHODS ARE THERE TO EMBRACE LOVE?

- First embrace yourself, and then love will flow through you.

- Transform any fears you may have. See chapter *"Fear."*

- Do not judge others or yourself, love cannot be present when judgement is.

- Change negative thoughts into positive thoughts, then you will become more present.

- Unconditional love means to have no conditions to receive anything when giving. It is being without Ego.

I say no
to old thought
patterns

WHAT DOES IT MEAN TO SAY NO TO OLD THOUGHT
PATTERNS?

Saying no to old thought patterns is an opportunity to open up and receive life in a different way. This is especially important if you have a feeling that you are "stuck" or that nothing is moving forward. It is not about denying anything, but seeing things in a different light. The opportunities are reachable when you are willing to say no to your old thought patterns. It is however important that you have a desire to receive these opportunities, or else very little will happen. An old thought pattern can be emotionally based and have strong connections to fear. You are, by saying no to the fear and the old thoughts, helping to transform the emotional energy and old thinking patterns. In this way you are rewiring your mind by blocking the receptors to the old thought patterns and you are instead creating new ones. This can help you connect more strongly to your intuitive and innovative qualities. See also chapter *"Rewiring your mind."*

WHAT HAPPENS WITHIN YOU WHEN YOU SAY NO TO
OLD THOUGHT PATTERNS?

Old thought patterns can keep you locked in the past. By saying no, new opportunities can arise since you are prepared to go where you may not have wanted to go before. This may take you into new areas and new ventures simply by letting go of your old thoughts. By saying no to old thought patterns you are:

• Denying the Ego from having its own way again and again.

• Helping to transform your emotional energies that can interfere with your thought patterns.

• Transforming your fear into trust.

• Freeing yourself from external control factors.

• Building greater confidence in your Self.

The effect of the above is that "your old consciousness" cannot control you anymore and you will empower your thoughts towards positive awareness.

WHAT HAPPENS IN YOUR ENVIRONMENT WHEN YOU SAY NO TO OLD THOUGHT PATTERNS?

There may be others around you that are caught up in the old ways of thinking. If you change, then they may react with dislike and judge, fight or block anything that touches the innovative idea from entering the workplace. By saying no to some of the old thought patterns you may be the first one to take the positive step that is required for all to move on from old concepts and thought patterns. Change comes from within. When you as an individual or a whole group decide to step out of old thought patterns, then real change will come!

HOW DO PEOPLE SAYING NO TO OLD THOUGHT PATTERNS INFLUENCE A WORKING ENVIRONMENT?

If you are willing to take the opportunity to say no to the strong concepts and beliefs that seem to keep the working environment in old patterns, then positive change can happen. Whenever you say no to something, there has to be an alternative energy that can fill that space. When you say no to old thought patterns you are actually saying yes to something new. Many people would like to know what this 'new' is. But in some situations you may have to say no to your old thoughts and behaviour without knowing the answer to what should fill that space. This is when true innovative ideas can be created. Stay present and work with your intuition and you may receive an idea that is connected to a really innovative concept.

WHAT METHODS ARE THERE TO SAY NO TO OLD THOUGHT PATTERNS?

- Express your truth. It will help you release old fears that you may be holding on to.

- Say no to thoughts that you do not like. See chapter *"Rewiring your mind."*

- Investigate if the thoughts belong to you or if they possibly belong to someone else, then you will have adopted them as your own. In such a case give these thoughts back to the person they belong to.

- Transform your fears. Fears control mental and emotional behaviour. See chapter *"Fear."*

WHAT DOES IT MEAN TO SPEAK YOUR TRUTH WITH CLARITY?

Truth is a quality of light and nothing that is shared in truth can be hidden, changed or altered. The clarity of your truth is determined by your understanding of what truth represents for you. You communicate your truth through your messages of thoughts, words and action. They should not be clouded by your emotions. When you speak your truth with clarity, then it touches the hearts and minds of others. They intuitively know and feel the truth. Truth is releasing a positive force from within. It is a soul quality that is expressed through the spoken word as wisdom.

WHAT HAPPENS WITHIN YOU WHEN YOU SPEAK YOUR TRUTH?

It is an opportunity to share your deepest beliefs with others. By being true to your feelings and intuition you will find the strength to share your inner truth with others. One follows the other. Whenever you share your truth with others you are taking positive steps towards empowering yourself with greater light and this will be uplifting. Truth is your power and its release can transform any doubts you have about yourself. Truth is love. Your spirit and soul are activated through you expressing your truth. Your truth is your integrity and your integrity is an inner quality of believing in what you feel is right.

WHAT HAPPENS IN YOUR ENVIRONMENT WHEN YOU SPEAK YOUR TRUTH?

Speaking your truth will encourage others. If you are an example of truth then you are being a leader, a light for others to follow. This will have a very positive effect on everyone who shares your space as well as on those who may not be directly in touch with you. To be clear, precise and direct with your truth has values that everyone in your environment will feel in their psyche. Yes, it is a positive force whichever way you may look at it.

HOW DO PEOPLE WHO SPEAK THEIR TRUTH INFLUENCE A WORKING ENVIRONMENT?

Clarity brings clarity and truth attracts truth. Wherever such power is shared, then there will be light. Whenever there is light, there is joy. Yes, the clearly communicated truth is uplifting and it gives energy. To lie to others takes energy from the environment. What is hidden is not of the light and can therefore not be true!

WHAT METHODS ARE THERE FOR ME TO SPEAK MY TRUTH WITH CLARITY?

* Be true to yourself and then you will also be true to others. This is the first and most fundamental point to understand about your Self.

- Be clear about what it is you wish to share. Make sure that you understand the complete message before communicating.

- Truth is always simple. Do not complicate things by over-expanding on what you wish to share. Communicate in a simple way.

- Do not exaggerate or inflate your message. It is here that the Ego can step in to corrupt the truth of soul expression.

- Speak from your heart and truth will be there also, because the message of love carries integrity and understanding.

WHAT DOES IT MEAN TO TAKE RESPONSIBILITY FOR YOUR ACTIONS?

Being responsible for your actions means that you become accountable for your actions - one should naturally follow the other. It also means that you are being true to your Self. It is here that a greater sense of integrity can be accomplished within your work. This may give you a "feel good feeling." This could also mean saying no to something, like a task or to how someone may be treating you. The opposite of not taking responsibility for your actions can be when you are in denial of a mistake that you have made. Then you will pass it on to another who may have to fix it, or they may even be blamed for your mistake.

WHAT HAPPENS WITHIN YOU WHEN YOU TAKE RESPONSIBILITY FOR YOUR ACTIONS?

When you take responsibility for something it means that you manage it in a way that is true to the experience and that is caring for others. You build confidence in yourself as well as others. The accountability will encourage you to be more vigilant.

WHAT HAPPENS IN YOUR ENVIRONMENT WHEN YOU TAKE RESPONSIBILITY?

By taking responsibility for your actions the whole environment may change, as this is a positive force. Others will find that they can rely on you because you are true to the work you do, and others may seek guidance or help from you. When you are being responsible for your actions you will find that you become more present in what you are doing. It will also encourage you to do the best that you can with greater joy.

HOW DO PEOPLE THAT TAKE RESPONSIBILITY INFLUENCE A WORKING ENVIRONMENT?

If everyone takes responsibility for themselves and their actions, the ethos of the working environment will be a positive one. Nothing would be hidden or put onto someone else as a means of escaping blame or fault. Greater respect would be held for one another. Imagine that the whole workforce were accountable, nothing would be stolen or hidden. Things would not be locked up because truth and respect would become the norm for other people's property and what they share.

WHAT METHODS ARE THERE TO EMBRACE RESPONSIBILITY FOR YOUR ACTIONS?

• Be true to yourself. See chapter *"The Self."*

• Admit mistakes.

- When you decide to be accountable for your actions, responsibility is no longer an issue because you are managing in a holistic way.

- Be true to whatever you are doing. Then it becomes a matter of fact to admit when something has gone wrong, or that you have made a mistake.

WHAT DOES IT MEAN TO TAKE RESPONSIBILITY FOR
YOUR FEELINGS?

It is important to recognise that your feelings will take you
to your light. This can be experienced when your feelings
awaken your emotions, giving you opportunity to transform
them. The acceptance and transformation of your emotions
will have a deep positive influence on your thinking. By
not being lost in your emotions you are no longer affected
or influenced by them. You can turn around any negative
response or feeling that you have, simply by recognising
that it is there. By accepting the feelings you have, you take
responsibility for them. Feelings come and go, we receive and
give feelings equally. This must mean that we are equally
responsible for what we give out on a feeling level, as well
as what we take in. Feelings are there to help take you to the
light. You should first understand them and then transform
any controlling factors that are negatively connected to them.
In this way you will manage the feelings that you receive
from others. If you are being true to your feelings then you
are being true to their expression. When you are true to your
feelings you take responsibility for them. When you are not
true to your feelings, then the Ego is in control.

WHAT HAPPENS WITHIN YOU WHEN YOU TAKE RESPONSIBILITY FOR YOUR FEELINGS?

When you take responsibility for your feelings and are true to them, then real progress is being made in transforming them. The true feeling – such as an intuitive thought – will feel right, and if acted upon will produce positive results. If on the other hand you are holding onto a negative feeling, that negative force will not be in harmony with your intuitive quality and will continue to hold you in the negative. By being responsible for any negative feeling you may have, you can begin to look for ways in which to transform the negative energy into a positive force, instead of passing it on to others. As positive progress is made in this area you may find that you gradually begin to take things less personally. You will not be so offended by another person's opinion of you or what you may be sharing. Life becomes less complicated.

WHAT HAPPENS IN YOUR ENVIRONMENT WHEN YOU TAKE RESPONSIBILITY FOR YOUR FEELINGS?

Being responsible in any aspect of life is to be positive, but being responsible for one's feelings is indeed a big step to take. Within this responsibility you may decide not to pass on any negative feelings to another. If, for example, you are delivering something to a colleague and are in a negative mode, that person will certainly feel your energy and may even step back from you – an unconscious happening. This is because they are protecting themselves from your negative energy; but by taking responsibility you may avoid feeling sorry for yourself and put some joy into what you are doing instead.

HOW DO PEOPLE TAKING RESPONSIBILITY FOR THEIR FEELINGS INFLUENCE A WORKING ENVIRONMENT?

As you learn to manage your feelings, the positive force will touch others on an energy level. When this occurs then those around you will feel more relaxed because you are. As feelings are transformed from negative into positive forces, the feeling of a working environment will follow a positive line. The area may feel lighter, particularly if many within a working environment have transformed their own feelings in a positive way.

WHAT METHODS ARE THERE TO TAKE RESPONSIBILITY FOR YOUR FEELINGS?

Here are a few guidelines that will help you transform your feelings:

- Understand which feelings are yours. You may be carrying other people's feelings, such as anger or sadness. You will intuitively know which are yours. The feelings which are not yours will interfere with your own energy in a number of ways. If you feel confused or have doubts, then this is a sign that you should investigate whether the feeling belongs to you or another person. See chapter *"Doubt."*

- Seek ways to turn and transform negative feelings into positive ones. See chapters *"I say no to old thought patterns"* and *"I accept."*

- If you feel that you may have offended or hurt another person through negative expressions of your feelings, then try to put it right as soon as you can. Do not wait for tomorrow to say sorry or apologise.

- Do not look for solutions outside of yourself or blame someone else for the way you feel. The change starts from within. See chapters *"Projections"* and *"I accept."*

- Developing your intuition will help you become more trusting of your inner feelings so that you can trust. See chapter *"Intuition."*

- Being fully present means you will enter all experiences with your whole Self, and that means to trust. See chapter *"I am present."*

- Transform your fears and you will be able to trust. See chapter *"Fear."*

- Learn to say no and to express your views and you will become more trusting of your Self.

- Think positively and you will become more trusting of what is to come.

- If you find it difficult to trust others, then have a look at what it is that you do not trust in your Self.

WHAT DOES IT MEAN TO BE NEUTRAL?

Being neutral to any given situation means that you take no sides; you do not get involved in the mental or emotional battle. Some would call it "sitting on the fence." It means that you are unbiased. All referees are meant to be neutral and as such hold that level of consciousness and respect for the game they referee. It also means that you do not intrude until you feel it is right to express your view. You share your truth in a balanced and neutral manner. This could be called insight with integrity.

WHAT HAPPENS WITHIN YOU WHEN YOU ARE NEUTRAL?

When you are neutral then you are not judging the situation or another person. You are simply observing what is taking place. From that position you are able to observe from a non-judgemental viewpoint. The Ego is not influencing you because you are managing to be calm and neutral. You are the observer and will be more aware of what is taking place. You will be able to share your thoughts with neutrality. You will see the bigger picture and will decide what the correct course of action is. Here is an example: the medicine man of a Native American group holds great respect from all the people of that tribe. The reason is that the medicine man is always neutral; this means that you cannot say to him, "hey, I will give you three of my best horses if you give your blessings for me to marry the daughter of Running Bear." The medicine man will refuse such an offer because he holds deep integrity, and as such cannot be corrupted by material possessions as they have no meaning or purpose for him. Everyone in the tribe knows this and therefore trusts and respects his view, advice and wisdom because he is neutral.

WHAT HAPPENS IN YOUR ENVIRONMENT WHEN YOU ARE NEUTRAL?

When you are neutral in your workplace the reactions of others around you may vary. Some will not know how to deal with you when you do not take sides in a work matter. Some may come to you to share their problems with an expectation that you may advise or judge the situation or a person that they may be complaining about. But if you do not buy into the drama, and do not offer a judgement that they may have expected from you to be in their favour, you may be ignored by that person for a while. On the other hand, others may respect your neutrality and seek advice with the knowledge that you are unbiased and cannot be corrupted or influenced by others or your own motives.

HOW DO PEOPLE THAT ARE NEUTRAL INFLUENCE A WORKING ENVIRONMENT?

Not all people in a working environment are neutral to the events that are taking place within it, but those who are usually hold a healthy amount of respect from others within that workplace. It is a positive force that is carried by those who remain neutral in all happenings. Whenever judgement is not present, the greater force of truth is.

- Become non-judgemental.

- Accept things as they are. Your acceptance of a situation is needed even if you want to create change in that situation or what is behind it. Acceptance will help you towards being neutral. See chapter "*I accept.*"

- Learn to be present and you will learn to be still. In stillness you see and feel more without getting involved. See chapter "*I am present.*"

- Improve your listening skills. You are the observer. The one who does not speak, listens and learns!

Trust and Intuition

SAY GOODBYE TO FEAR!

One of the happiest moments in my life was when I stood in the sun looking over a field of beautiful flowers. I do not know why this feeling came over me. Everything was chaos in my life but I felt, for a few moments, a very peaceful and warm feeling in my heart. It felt like my life just stopped. I can still recall this feeling years later. This is where I would like to be, all of the time!

I totally agree with you! You describe the feeling you experience when you are in contact with your inner joy, peace and love! And I know you can be there all the time!

That is hard to believe. I have tried to relive the feeling many times, but I am not able to. And I have spent many sleepless nights thinking about what it is that I need to do in order to get back to that feeling.

Nothing!

Nothing? But how can I get there?

That is the whole point. You are trying to achieve something that you already have inside. Learn to be who you are!

I am not sure I am following you here.

Do you remember that we already talked about joy, peace, love and light being inside of you?

Yes, I remember that.

The situation you described was a moment when you had full access to that, but you still have fears clouding your view and you still have that need to control what is happening in your life. That is why you so seldom get access to those inner feelings of joy, love and peace.

Yes, I know. I am afraid that I will fail in my job.

So you worry that you will not be good enough at work?

Yes, and I also see my colleagues laugh when I make a fool of myself.

So you visualise your colleagues laughing at you after you have failed? Has this happened to you before, someone laughing at you?

No, not at work, but I remember when I was in school and my classmates were laughing at me because I said something stupid when the teacher asked about our homework. That picture keeps coming back to me.

So this is one way that fear has a grip on you. You have a negative past experience and you would like to make your future safe to avoid that happening again?

Yes, I would like to avoid that happening in the future. It was such a horrible experience.

But is it happening?

No, not yet...

Move yourself to the present moment! Concentrate on what is happening in the now. This is the one place where fear cannot exist! And when you manage to keep yourself present in the moment, you do not need to control the future. You will learn to trust. And when you trust and are in the moment, then your fears will gradually disappear.

That sounds nice! I actually think that I will start right away! But it also sounds a bit scary. Is it really true that I can become fearless?

Of course you can! You can manage whatever comes your way. In fact you always have! It is how you read your experiences that determine how you feel about them. See them as teachers for growth. Try to look at them from a different perspective and do not take things that happen in your life personally. Nothing is ever personal – you are just having an experience.

I think that I will need some help with the interpretation of my experiences. Can you please do that with me?

Thank you for inviting me! I have always been here and cannot wait to start work with you. I am thrilled! Just imagine the power we hold when we combine our forces. Logic and intuition. Wow! From now on, let's agree that everything we do, we do from the heart, because where love is, fear cannot be!

The Ego
Doubt
Rejection
Identity
Escape
Speculation
Projections
Guilt
Worry
Protection
Past
Experiences
Fear
Expectations
Anger
Stress
Denial
Pain

Print your personal copy of the Fear and Control clouded view
on *www.sensitelligent.com*.

FEAR AND CONTROL

Fear and Control

Anger

WHAT IS ANGER?

Anger has a deep connection to (old) emotions that are stored in your body. It can be a result of past experiences where the feelings connected to these experiences are hidden or stored. You will also often experience anger when you have expectations of yourself and others, especially when you find that those expectations are not met. The Ego uses anger to defend itself by attacking another. Anger can also be a way of controlling others through fear. See also the chapter "*Ego.*"

HOW DOES ANGER WORK?

Anger arises within in an effort to control or defend. It follows two paths. The first path is to try and influence others by demonstrating power through the spoken word or by physical means. An example can be when someone is not happy with the work that you are doing and they become angry with you. But ask yourself; are they actually angry with me? The answer is never, they are angry with themselves. You are simply a way for the anger to be released. The basis for this is mostly to be found in the frustration within themselves. It is often connected to an expectation of some kind. It could be as simple as you being late for an appointment or a target that has to be met at a specific time. The one who is in charge of the situation may then become angry and verbally abuse you. Verbal abuse either tries to make you feel bad or seeks to give you a guilt complex in order for it not to happen again. Either way, the person who is angry at you is actually doing it to their own self - they know this on a subconscious level, but they often cannot stop their reaction.

The second path is activated when the emotions take priority over the mind. This side of anger is often hidden more deeply within the person as a mental energy and the energy is often connected to a past experience that still is fearful to that person. When the emotions take priority over the mind, then you become an emotional thinker. An emotional thinker can be like gunpowder that can explode at the smallest intrusive vibration. For example, anger can rise up in another person if you share your truth about that person or the situation. You may have pushed a button that awakens their anger. The angry reaction is very likely to be a response from the Ego – because it does not want to hear the truth. It is attacking you as a natural defence.

HOW DOES MY ANGER INFLUENCE MY WORK?

If you are holding any form of anger it will flow into everything that you are creating or touching. Anger is an energy thought form that must go somewhere. For example, let us say that you are at home and you are building a small stone wall in the garden. You are very angry about a situation at work. You mix the cement and start to build the wall under the premise of your anger. Every stone that you lay in that wall will be holding an angry vibration because your consciousness is connected to the work that you are doing, it is not separated from your feelings. When the wall is finished and is dry and strong, you may find that no one wants to be near the wall. This is because subconsciously they pick up on the negative vibrations of your anger that is now stored in every stone in the wall. This is how energy works and how a strong negative force like anger can affect your workplace.

HOW DO ANGRY PEOPLE INFLUENCE THE WORK ENVIRONMENT?

If anyone is angry in a workplace then the whole environment can become negative. Others will feel the anger directly or indirectly. If an angry person has been sitting on a seat where you just sat down, then you may begin to feel uncomfortable sitting there and you may even choose to change seats. You move because you feel the angry energy that was left in the fabric of the chair. You may find it difficult to share or be open with a person who is angry, even if you do not show it openly, but rather avoid the person or the situation. This is natural as you will probably interpret their anger as danger. Others in the environment will also feel the vibration, and are likely to avoid rather than choose to meet the angry person. The person who is angry will fail to inspire others and will make them close down.

HOW TO TRANSFORM ANGER?

Here are some basic steps that will be helpful if you carry anger:

- The first step is to recognise that you have anger. The fact that you recognise that you are angry will start the inner healing – especially if you also express a wish to understand the underlying causes for your anger. See chapters *"I accept"* and *"I take responsibility for my feelings."*

- Be true to yourself and you will find that you will automatically be true to others. You will have less anger when you are true to yourself. Ask what there is to be angry about. See chapter "*I trust.*"

- Study how you react in all life situations. Maybe you would like to change the ways you respond to others in order to be true to yourself? Reflecting and changing the way you respond will make you more responsible for your actions. See chapter "*I take responsibility for my actions.*"

- Do not take anything personally. When this quality is mastered then you will enter all experiences without judgement. This will, in a calm manner, allow you to accept any situation you may find yourself in. You will find that this will complement the situation and not attack it. See chapter "*I accept.*"

- Be present. When you have learned to be present then you will be fully living in the now. The past and the future will have no control over your mind, body and emotions. See chapter "*I am present.*"

IF YOU MEET AN ANGRY PERSON – HOW CAN YOU HELP?

- The first step is to acknowledge that the person is angry. The fact that you say that you have noticed that a person is angry will start the transformation of the situation. You can just confirm that you feel that the person is angry/upset/irritated. See chapter "*I accept.*"

- Be true to yourself. Try not to take in the anger. Stay with what is true within you. See chapter "*I trust.*"

- Study your response. Try not to get caught in the other person's aggression. Always respond in a calm way.

Remember that anger feeds anger. See chapter "*I take responsibility for my actions.*"

- Do not take anything personally. When you stop taking things personally, then you will be able to accept any situation you may find yourself in. And you will find that this will help you calm down the situation rather than attack it. It will also help bring the angry person back to their senses. See chapter "*I accept.*"

- Be present. When you are fully present then you do not get caught in your past experiences and feelings. You will also not fear what comes next. It is then impossible for the other person's anger to have an impact on you. See chapter "*I am present.*"

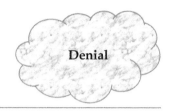
Denial

WHAT IS DENIAL?

Denial is based on your fears, and your fears are based on the denial of your truth. In this respect you are denying your power of light, truth, joy and love. Saying no to someone is different from denying that person something. "No" sends a clear message. With denial there can be hidden factors, such as not liking a person or denying that you are good at something and therefore setting yourself up for failure rather than success.

HOW DOES DENIAL AFFECT YOU?

If you fear your truth then you deny your higher Self. This is predominantly about your power of light and not the power of the physical will and Ego. Whenever you are in denial you are running away or hiding from your inner power and truth. Which power you use, the Ego's power or your higher truth create the experience in your life. You always attract to yourself what you need to learn. Your denial is showing you what, and often why you are avoiding something. Denial has a connection to doubt. If you doubt yourself, you may well deny yourself an opportunity to experience something new because you have a fear connected to it.

HERE ARE SOME EXAMPLES OF DENIAL:

• You deny your truth.

• You deny your power.

• You do not stand strong and face wrongdoing.

• You do not have the courage to speak when no one else is speaking.

• You do not dare to express your feelings and thoughts about a situation.

HOW DOES MY DENIAL INFLUENCE MY WORK?

When you are in denial at work then you are affecting your work by:

• Being afraid to meet people.

• Being afraid to share your thought.

• Being afraid to say no to something or someone that you feel is not right.

• Other people may find it difficult to respect you because you are not clear about work issues.

HOW DO PEOPLE WHO DENY INFLUENCE THE WORK ENVIRONMENT?

Can you imagine what a working environment would be like if the majority of the workforce were in denial? Little progress would be made because confusion would be present rather than clarity. Denial is present when you are unsure. And if you get a lot of unsure people in an environment, those people will not know where they stand or who they can trust. This is a negative energy that will bring down the positive energy that may be there.

HOW TO TRANSFORM DENIAL?

• Constantly watch your emotional and mental response to a situation. Do you feel good inside at all times? When you do not, what is it that you do not feel good about?

• Transform any fears you may be carrying. See chapter "*Fear.*"

• Rediscover the power of being your Self. See chapter "*The Self.*"

• Find the courage to be true to yourself and others. See chapter "*I trust.*"

Doubt

WHAT IS DOUBT?

Whenever doubt is present, so is fear. The energy of doubt appears whenever you are not sure of something, and when you are not sure then mental confusion is present. Mental confusion is based upon fear; the fear of taking a positive decision creates doubt. Fear has its roots in a past experience that in some way prevents you from being present. This blocks you from trusting that the decision you are going to make is the right one. Fear is often connected to the concept of failure. This can be emotionally based. When someone always seems to doubt themselves time after time they find it difficult to make a positive decision, this is known in Britain as the "Doubting Thomas." The doubting Thomas holds the energy of all the above, and although this is not a fault in itself, there is a distinct lack of trust to move forward.

HOW DOES DOUBT AFFECT YOU?

What is the hesitation about that makes you doubt yourself? Doubt prevents you from being present. Whenever you are not being present you are not in your power. You are not truly serving when you are in doubt, because confusion is present where trust should be. Your doubting can have a negative effect on others. If you are not confident about where you are in any given moment and doubt steps in, then you can understand that this may confuse others around you to. If you are holding another person's doubt then you are also sharing their responsibility from an energy point of view. This can spread though the workforce of a company and create a negative effect in all areas.

HOW DOES MY DOUBTING INFLUENCE MY WORK?

Doubt can influence all aspects of your life, but in your workplace it can be particularly sensitive. If for example you doubt your ability to be creative, the message you send to yourself is "I am not worthy" or "I will fail." By thinking in this way you have psychologically failed from within yourself. This is because by doubting, the Ego has taken your power away in an effort to control you. It does this by giving more identity to your negative belief system. Your doubting Thomas will continue to control you, until you decide to change. When that change happens your working pattern will be less cloudy and greater clarity will develop from within yourself.

HOW DO PEOPLE WHO DOUBT INFLUENCE THE WORK ENVIRONMENT?

In most working environments there are set rules and criteria that govern how a company is organised and run. Due to this fact every individual working within that environment to some degree affects the other. For example, if a colleague informs you one day that they have made up their mind about a concept that you are both involved in, and the next day that person calls you and says that they are now not sure - how would that impact you? If you have a number of people whose behaviour patterns are similar, then projects will slow down or even stop due to the confusion that doubt creates.

- Transform you fears and you will be more present. You doubting yourself will become less and less. See chapter *"Fear."*

- Try to stay with your initial feeling. You can be over-analytical about a decision that you may need to make, and the mind goes round and round, looking for answers. This can create doubts. See chapter *"I follow my inner compass."*

- Trust your intuitive quality when making decisions and doubt will disappear. A strong positive decision can be made. See chapter *"I follow my inner compass."*

- Tell yourself "I can hold and manage any experience that comes my way." This is good for self-empowerment. See chapter *"I stay open to receive the unexpected."*

- Believe in your Self. See chapter *"The Self."*

Fear and Control

Escape

WHAT DOES IT MEAN TO ESCAPE?

Escapism – apart from physical survival - is the result of fear. It is good to remember that avoidance is also an aspect of escaping. Escape has three forms that you may see or experience in everyday life. These are the physical, emotional and mental forms of escape.

PHYSICAL ESCAPE has many forms. It can be for example to avoid a serious accident and therefore escape injury. Breaking free from jail is another way to physically escape. To face someone physically can be challenging and is often avoided due to fear. You may literally walk around a person at work in order to either avoid him/her seeing you, or you seeing them.

EMOTIONAL ESCAPE can be difficult to recognise if you are an emotional person. The emotional escape usually seeks a reward of some kind. One of the most common forms of emotional escape is through food, i.e. overeating. Another is through alcohol. Another is compulsive buying. Yet another common emotional escape is to put you in the drama scenario in order to attract attention to yourself. This is an emotional attempt to receive pity or comfort from another colleague or friend. Anger is in many cases used as a means of escape, but is often not recognised as such.

MENTAL ESCAPE could be as simple as to delude the memory by forgetting a name; this is a form of escape. You may not want to get into a conversation with a specific person and as such will continually escape by avoiding that conversation. We escape our responsibility by putting the blame on someone else. We point our finger towards another and in this way tell them that it was their fault not ours. You may be dishonest in order to avoid the truth or for the truth not to be shown. Lying is a common form of escape that can have far reaching consequences, but the truth will eventually always be seen.

WHAT HAPPENS WITHIN YOU WHEN YOU ESCAPE?

When you find yourself escaping it is usually down to a fear of some kind. The unpredictable, unknown and unexpected can and do create stress if fear is not transformed from within the Self. Here are some examples of escape:

- You may fear and avoid the unknown by not venturing into something new, such as a new project or assignment.

- You may hold on to the old and known ways until pushed into the unknown by something outside of your control.

- You may be escaping taking responsibility for your actions.

- You may be escaping your inner truth.

- You may be escaping your inner power.

- You may be escaping being successful.

- You may be escaping the possibility of failure.

Whenever you escape you are always taking yourself into the past or future. Both are traps that will keep you in the energies of fear, doubt, speculation and judgement. Lack of Self respect can be the reason why a person continually escapes their responsibilities.

WHAT HAPPENS IN YOUR ENVIRONMENT WHEN YOU ESCAPE?

Whenever you are escaping you are never present, therefore you cannot be adding a positive energy to the aura or atmosphere of the place. In fact the opposite will occur. By escaping you cannot plant your personality there for it to grow and flourish. You are not present, you are lost. And those who know you on another level will also feel your lack of presence. They may ask "where are you today?"

HOW DO PEOPLE WHO ESCAPE INFLUENCE A WORKING ENVIRONMENT?

The workforce itself becomes unbalanced. Without a strong foundation of truth, trust and tenacity that shows the quality of being determined to do something with firm purpose, then the energy of the working environment will be negative. In order to build an aura of trust in any working environment the workforce within that environment must individually hold the essence of the three T's – truth, trust and tenacity. One follows the other, but it first starts within each and everyone. Be inspired by a work colleague by all means, but inspire yourself to inspire others and the message of escape will no longer be present. The opposite is corruption.

- Whenever you find yourself avoiding something, stop and ask; why am I escaping? What is it that I do not like about myself? What is it that I fear? Watch your thoughts constantly. See chapter *"Fear."*

- Take responsibility for your feelings and be accountable. See chapter *"I take responsibility for my feelings."*

- Take responsibility for your actions and be accountable. See chapter *"I take responsibility for my actions."*

- Be true to what you believe to be your truth.

- Learn to say no to any fears you may have by facing your inner truth. See chapters *"I trust" and "Fear."*

Expectations

WHAT ARE EXPECTATIONS?

It is here that one touches upon the future. All expectations are futuristic in their outlook. When you are expecting you are waiting for something to happen rather than being present in the moment. Expectations are often based on needs, and needs are often to be found in our insecurities about ourselves and others. This can be a hidden factor that you may not be aware of or admit to yourself. Expectations are based on needs whereas visions are in touch with your creativity and intuition. Visions will help you move forward in accordance with your truth. See chapter "*Dreams and Visions.*"

HOW DO EXPECTATIONS AFFECT YOU?

If you have any kind of expectation about anything, then you are setting yourself up for disappointment. As an example, let us say that you are expecting a phone call at 15.00 from your friend Lisa who said she would call you then. Another friend, Sam, calls you and asks you to come over to his place for late lunch. You say that you cannot come because you are expecting a phone call from a friend, and that you do not want to miss it. You stay in and wait for the call. Time passes by, it is now 15.15 and you wait a bit longer. It is now 15.30, and you continue to wait. You have no way of contacting Lisa because she has a new phone number. But as time moves on you become more agitated about your friend not calling you. It is now 16.00 and you decide not to wait any longer and go out for a walk. You return home at 17.00 and as you come through the door the phone rings, it is Lisa. She apologises about not calling you at 15.00. She explains that Sam called unexpectedly with a picnic lunch that they enjoyed in the garden. The question here is who missed what?

Expectations can also be connected to power issues. For example by the setting of targets that are impossible to meet. There is a subtle energy exchange taking place that puts the emphasis upon the ones who have been given the job to reach those expected goals. This aspect puts pressure and stress upon the workers who are expected to achieve the target. Expectations take you away from your power because they keep you trapped in future probabilities and possibilities. As you are waiting for something to arrive, you lose energy doing it, because somewhere that thought and feeling is active through your expectations. Another clear example of how expectations can lead to conflict is by promising someone something. You will automatically lead them into the expectation mode, and if not delivered on time or in the way that was expected, some form of conflict may occur, if the situation is not fully accepted by the receiver. If you are waiting for something to arrive, why give it energy when it has not yet arrived? An example could be if you expect a salary increase, you hope you will get it (you are not in control) and you speculate how big it is going to be (expectation). Furthermore, if there is a negative energy attached to it then it may well have a negative effect on you and the situation.

HOW DO MY EXPECTATIONS INFLUENCE MY WORK?

The most important aspect is that any form of expectation keeps you from being fully present. This may have a negative effect upon your efficiency and decision making. Whenever you are not present you are being inefficient. Furthermore, if you are expecting something you may delay or even put on hold something else because you are expecting an answer, which may not even come at the desired or expected time. Such common scenarios create much stress in working environments.

HOW DO PEOPLE'S EXPECTATIONS INFLUENCE THE WORK ENVIRONMENT?

A business can have great expectations, but ask yourself who is supposed to be doing the work – is it you and your colleagues? Your collective expectations can lead you and others in your work environment towards another illusion, that of hope. This often occurs when you do not trust that you will reach your objectives, but you hope to get there. Then those in the workplace are influenced by expectation, hope and speculation. Speculation can create a false sense of security, if for example you expect you will get money tomorrow and you already spend it today. Can you see the downturn that is taking place here? These are energies that can produce a negative effect in any working environment.

HOW TO TRANSFORM EXPECTATIONS

Expectations are built into the very fabric of today's societies, and much stress is caused by them. This is mainly due to the time factor that is connected to any form of expectation.

Here are some ways in which you may eliminate the concept of expectation:

- Learn to be present. It will teach you to avoid expectations. This way of thinking automatically takes you away from the distraction of expectancies from yourself or others within your working and home environment. See chapter *"I am present."*

- Strive towards the vision, but continually evaluate the time aspect of the goals. It is one thing to strive to meet certain goals or ideas with good intent, but it is another to be motivated through achieving. Then great expectancy is placed upon your shoulders which can create a lot of negative stress.

- Focus on the right intent by being creative and innovative. Try to transform the concept of achieving into one of trusting that things will be right. When you have the right intentions you are in your power of "being while doing." You are not focussed on expectations. This will make it possible to stay in "the flow."

Fear

WHAT IS FEAR?

Fear is old energy that was created to help protect all human beings from danger. Fear has a strong link to the natural instinct of survival that is based in the lower consciousness. There are two forms of fear. The first being your natural instinct of survival, the second being Ego-based. Ask yourself what is the difference between the instincts of survival and the Ego's fear. For example the survival fears will tell you when it is not safe to cross the road, or when a danger is connected to an open fire. The Ego's fear is an illusion that floods the lower mind and confuses the natural instincts of fear. The lower-mind fears what it cannot see or understand and that is why it does not like changes to occur. From the logic the world is viewed as being black or white. Logic wants to control all things and the Ego creates fear so that nothing will be changed. This is why fears that are Ego-based are the greatest protector of the Ego itself.

HOW DOES FEAR AFFECT YOU?

Ego-based fear is your greatest controlling factor. It seeks to separate you from trusting yourself and then it is not possible to trust others. The Ego's form of fear tries to prevent you from being intuitive. It will tell your logic that what you experience when using your intuition is not true. It will say to you that this is only your imagination. This is just one example of how fear creates separation. Fear prevents you from walking into the unknown, which could mean that you cannot let go of something or someone because you do not trust yourself. Fear often prevents you from listening to your intuition and accepting higher consciousness where wisdom and knowledge can be found. This is because intuition is not a logical energy form. It is of higher consciousness. When you are being intuitive you are being spiritual and when you are being spiritual you are being intuitive. Fear tries to break your connection to your higher consciousness in order to prevent you from being intuitive and spiritual.

Fear stirs up emotional energies to make them seem bigger than what they really are. When you let go of your fears then you are learning to trust your Self and the universe on a deeper level. The way you think is in this respect of great importance, because:

- You attract what you fear. If you focus on what you fear, then you will attract it. It is therefore important to change how you think about things. See chapter *"Rewiring your mind"* for some more insights into how to change your thought patterns.

- You often become angry because you have fear. It is a defence system that kicks in automatically when you fear something. Anger is a way of releasing hidden fear. See chapter *"Anger."*

- Fear drains the body of its vital life force by creating stress. The outer expression of stress can be connected to a deeper hidden factor of fear that is creating the stress itself.

HOW DOES MY FEAR INFLUENCE MY WORK?

Fear can prevent you from being creative, innovative and intuitive in your workplace. For example, you may fear sharing an idea because you feel that you may be stepping on someone else's toes. You do not want to disturb things so you may decide to play safe instead by keeping quiet out of fear of persecution on some level. You may not know it, but some of your fears may not be yours. A fear may in fact belong to someone else, but it can still heavily influence your work due to the negative vibration that is connected to that fear. Such a fear may confuse your decision making.

Another example of how fear is multiplied can be if you have been given an assignment for which you feel the time schedule is too short. You do not express your concerns during the meeting. Then the original thought of not speaking up about your concerns will create greater fear. This means that the fear has just doubled. You are holding the original fear of why you did not express your original concerns about the time factor, and secondly you now fear being late with the delivery of work that is expected of you. This is detrimental to your work as fear is now the motivating force, instead of joy and creativity.

HOW DOES PEOPLE'S FEAR INFLUENCE THE WORK ENVIRONMENT?

Can you imagine a workforce that is oriented by fear in order to achieve. Now imagine what the atmosphere of the working environment would feel like. You could probably cut it with a knife due to the level of stress that would be present. If you were to ask your colleagues what they feared in the workplace, what do you think their answer would be - I fear to be open, to share my insights, to speak my truth? In such a controlled environment the intuitive and innovative qualities of the workforce are being suppressed. The negative energy that fear holds will bring down the vibration of those who are working within that environment. The effects of which are often demonstrated by others having a lack of patience or being irritated and angry because they are under a great deal of negative stress.

HOW TO TRANSFORM FEAR?

Fear in any environment is a negative force that is in fact giving you the opportunity to do the opposite!

- Ask yourself what is it that you do not trust about yourself (instead of asking what it is you fear?). Work with yourself to build trust in areas where you feel fear. See chapter "*I trust.*"

- Watch how you respond in any given situation in life. Look at what the situation wants to show you and what opportunity you have been given to transform. Then you will be able to begin to make the necessary changes. One such change can be to go from negative- to positive thinking. See chapter "*Rewiring your mind.*"

- Take a step back and breathe deeply before you respond to another person. This is another way to start transforming your fears. Taking a deep breath and stepping back for a moment will give you space to adjust and to get another feeling of what is happening. Then your reaction may change. You may not react through fear and attack back, but seek wisdom through acceptance. See chapters "*I accept*" and "*I am present.*"

- Do not read the negative news in the newspaper or watch it on TV. A step in the right direction could be as simple as avoiding all the negative input. Fear is being built more and more into the very fabric of modern day life. Be disciplined to find a deeper quality of stillness in your life. Be on guard against what disturbs you.

- Realise that you cannot run away from your fears. You carry them wherever you go, until they are transformed from within into trust.

- Do not fear an experience, but embrace it instead. Fear is a dark energy that is only as real as your believe it to be. "Feel the fear, but do it anyway!" This will take you into your power of light. Light transforms the shadows of doubt that fear creates.

Fear and Control

Guilt

WHAT IS GUILT?

Guilt is a negative form of energy that comes from deep within your emotional body and can have a strong negative effect upon the mental body too. Guilt has a deep connection to your truth, feelings and emotions and are often linked to expectations of yourself and others. It is important to know that guilt is something that we create in ourselves. Guilt can be a motivating factor to make something right after you have misjudged a person or a situation. Your guilt will then guide you to seek forgiveness and acceptance when used correctly. There are two main areas from where we create the guilt feelings. Let us look more deeply into each one:

1. PAST EXPERIENCES

The guilt feeling can be linked to a past experience that you are holding on too. The self-created guilt may be due to a conditioning that you have received from childhood by your mother or father. They may have told something that made you feel inadequate. No matter what you did, it was never good enough for them. This can be carried into your adulthood, which demonstrates itself as lack of self-confidence, insecurity and indecisiveness. Guilt can also be created by feeling insecure about how you have reacted towards another person or situation. If for example your reaction was a negative one in which you lost your temper and verbally abused a colleague, you may feel guilty about it for days after.

2. EXPECTATIONS

The second cause of guilt is created by others who may seek to make you feel guilty about a situation in your workplace. Have you ever been told at work that what you achieved was not good enough, or not quick enough, or not in the right order? If fear has not already worked, then guilt can be used as a means to get more out of you. Your own expectations are the same but with the difference that you are the one setting the expectations on yourself and you are the judge of yourself. You may as an example feel that you have not worked hard enough to achieve something.

HOW DOES GUILT AFFECT YOU?

Guilt has a strong negative effect upon the emotional and mental energy fields that will irritate the central nervous system. Guilt is about blame, usually of the Self. It can take you into mild forms of depression. Guilt can be very energy draining. It is as if you are symbolically carrying the heavy weight of guilt on your shoulders. You may become moody due to the guilt you are carrying. Eventually all forms of guilt must surface to seek transformation, even after a number of years. It is never too late and there are people who have released their guilt in their very last breath of life. That is how far you can carry guilt before seeking forgiveness. If you are holding guilt, please try addressing it as soon as possible.

HOW DOES MY GUILT INFLUENCE MY WORK?

If you are holding the feeling of not being good enough or doing enough, that guilt can take you into overachievement in order to compensate. The overachieving person is looking for a reward of some kind. It could be a pat on the back with the words "great, you have finished in time" or it could be a monetary reward. It is not so essential what the reward is for that person, it is the feeling that arises when receiving the reward that matters. Guilt in this case is about being seen, a feeling of belonging to a group or company. This compensates momentarily for the lack of acceptance of your Self. No reward will over time be enough and you will always end up with an empty feeling inside.

HOW DO GUILTY PEOPLE INFLUENCE THE WORK ENVIRONMENT?

If someone is carrying guilt feelings in your workplace then others will feel its presence and it will definitely have a negative effect on everyone in that environment. The very nature of guilt lowers the energy in any environment where it is present. If you have two people working alongside each other that are burdened with guilt then little joy will be present. Such a presence may even influence others to behave in the same way.

HOW TO TRANSFORM GUILT?

- Ask yourself if the guilt is yours or if you have been receiving guilt that belongs to someone else? It can be that you have unknowingly taken on something that belongs to a family member or a colleague.

- Search your soul for the feelings that are connected to the guilt (for anything that is yours). Inner soul searching is required to transform the feelings that are connected to the guilt feeling. If for example you feel guilty about how you have treated someone, approach that person as soon as you have realised your error and apologise. This may be enough to heal what has occurred. Then look at why you acted in such a way in the first place. Is there an underlying pattern? If there is, look to change it!

- Look at what you do not accept about others. You can feel guilty about something you see in another person which is a behaviour that you do not accept about yourself. You may not realise that you also have this behaviour, but are reacting strongly to the mirror effect of another person's behaviour.

- Clear out things from the past. Guilt is often an energy form that comes from past experiences. Whenever you are holding on to such energy then a certain part of you is caught in the past. Search your soul for past experiences and see what they are telling you. This can be an underlying irritation that will eventually create ill health. Some people can carry guilt for most of their lives. Why does it have to be like that? If you are true to those feelings, then your guilt can be cleared by you. It can be as simple as making a phone call. See chapter *"Past experiences."*

Identity

WHAT IS IDENTITY?

Identity is a form of recognition. There are two forms of recognition and for reasons of simplicity let us call them the "lower and higher personalities".

THE LOWER PERSONALITY

This is based on the energy of logic (lower consciousness) that mainly works through the five physical senses of hearing, sight, smell, taste and touch. However there are another two energy bodies that relate strongly to the lower personality which are the emotional body and the Ego. These three energy forms together hold the identity of the lower personality. In this level of consciousness there may be very little awareness of spirituality (higher consciousness orientation) and the person may simply be living a life that is based on the third dimension. This in itself is fine as long as the emotional energies and the Ego are not interfering with the harmony of life. However if the emotional body and the Ego are more present than the logical aspect, then there can be many difficulties to overcome. Let us take a deeper look at these three energy forms: the forces of logic, emotion and Ego.

LOGIC – the logical force comes from the left hemisphere of the brain which is masculine in its nature. Masculine in this context is power. The logical thinkers often finds themselves boxed in by their own thoughts, not being able to step out of a belief system that has been built into their reality. The logic can be very strong in this respect and a person will often not change their thoughts even if proven wrong. Logical thinkers often look outside of themselves for answers. Their outlook upon life is analytical, linear, specific, time orientated, verbal language, judgemental and corresponds to beliefs.

EMOTIONAL BODY – the energy that makes up the emotional body is mainly based upon needs and fears. It is an energy field that feels every vibration (such as thought and sound) within its environment. It also has a strong connection to the logical side of the mind. The emotional body can under certain circumstances overpower the mind. Jealousy and judgements are two examples of when emotions take over from the mind. The needs of an individual can be very demanding upon the person's life force. If the needs are not met then this can cause a trauma for the person and for those around that person.

EGO – the vibration of the Ego has far-reaching effects upon the life of anyone who is dominated by it. The Ego is about identity. This is what the Ego seeks at all times. It is always trying to dominate and control everything and everyone through judgement. The Ego looks for outward appearances to achieve recognition or respect, which are based on materialism and physical form. Examples are clothes, physical body and facial appearance, car, house, job, earnings etc. The Ego will try to block your intuition because it cannot be in the present. It tries to hold you in the past and future by creating fears and illusions. This is mainly to confuse you, and this prevents you from trusting your higher self.

This has its roots in higher consciousness or your fourth dimensional thinking. The intuitive thinker (higher personality) views life from within the Self, which is from within the circle of life, our eternity. This view of life is quite different from the logical thinking which boxes itself into its own belief systems. The spirit and soul reside within this higher personality and are continually seeking to harmonise your life force through the powers of compassion and love, light and truth. These are some of the qualities of your higher personality. You can only reach these when being present, where the Ego and fear do not have a hold upon your psyche. Some of the qualities of the higher personality are tolerance, acceptance, peace, love and a non-judgemental approach to life. These are some of the energies that seek to transform the lower personality by overcoming the difficulties that come from the controlling lower consciousness. The higher personality is a blend of peaceful compassionate action that seeks to create through peace, joy, love and integrity.

HOW DOES MY IDENTITY AFFECT ANOTHER PERSON?

This is basically determined by how deeply involved you are with an individual. But collectively we are one identity, which is why the concept of "oneness" is so relevant in today's multi-cultural societies.

It is often said that our personalities rub off on each other. We know our children are deeply affected by our behavioural patterns. If you take that into adulthood, are we any different in our workplace? We often copy another person's behaviour patterns. Our identity runs deep in our psyche. It is held in many parts of ourselves, such as the mind and emotions. Here is an example: it is scientifically known that

Fear and Control

people, who have received another individual's organ in a transplant operation, often have changes in personal characteristics. It has been recorded that a vegetarian began to eat meat, and that another individual who had been passive and accepting began to be the opposite and became aggressive. How did such an energy exchange happen? Because energy is in all things, the organ that was used in the transplant also contained certain characteristics of the individual from whom it was taken i.e. the donor. So when we say that "our personalities rub off on each other" there lies a deep truth there. This is also true in any place you may find yourself in, be it at work or at home. We touch others in more ways than we can imagine. These influences can have subtle effects on those around us. Would you rather be sharing a space with an aggressive or a peaceful person, a positive or a negative thinker? You carry a vibration which is known as a "life force" wherever you go, and those around you feel it on some level. Whatever you identify yourself with will touch and have an effect on others.

HOW DOES MY IDENTITY INFLUENCE MY WORK?

Whether you hold a positive or negative identity will affect your work accordingly. Your consciousness and emotions will be imprinted on any object that you are touching. Imagine that you are handing in some papers concerning a project that you have been working on. That same morning you became upset and angry about a relationship. Some of that negative energy would be passed into the papers you had been working on. When you go to hand the papers over, the receiver of those papers may decide not to touch the papers for some time, and may even avoid them for some unknown reason. When the papers are finally picked up and read, the negative energy within the papers may be felt by the person reading them, which could have a negative effect to the substance of the papers. The lesson here is that whatever you identify yourself with, will in some way have an effect on your working and living environment.

HOW DOES PEOPLE'S IDENTITY INFLUENCE THE WORK ENVIRONMENT?

We cannot escape from who we are, but some try to hide their true identities. An identity escape can come in the form of lies or pretending to be someone we are not. The illusion of who you think you are in this respect can be short lived, because memory has a habit of betraying us at the exact moment that we require it. So if you or others around you are not being true to yourselves it will impact the working environment in negative ways. And a distinct lack of trust may develop within the group which is not good for any workforce or the environment.

HOW DO I TRANSFORM MY IDENTITY?

You can raise your consciousness by transforming your logical thinking to intuitive thinking. The logic and intuitive qualities become one. See chapter *"Three levels of consciousness' rising."* In this way you will begin to transform the Ego and the hold it has had over you. This very seldom happens overnight by taking a magic pill or two. It takes a greater sense of reasonability and discipline of the Self for the necessary changes to be made. Some of which are:

- Seeking ways which will bring a greater sense of peace into your life. Use for example meditation and breathing. See chapters *"How to meditate"* and *"Breathing techniques."*

- Transforming all negative thinking into positive thinking (it takes no more energy to think positively about something than it does to think negatively). See chapter *"I say no to old thought patterns."*

- Being true to your feelings and yourself. See chapter *"I take responsibility for my feelings."*

- Learn to overcome all your fears. See chapter *"Fear."*

- Learn to listen more deeply to your intuition. See chapters *"I follow my inner compass"* and *"Intuition."*

- Understand that nothing is personal, it is a message. See chapter *"I accept."*

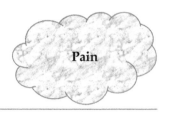

Pain

WHAT IS PAIN?

This is a deep subject to touch upon. Pain is for example felt when nerve endings are broken, such as when you cut yourself. Pain can also arise from a high level of emotional stimulation. Negative stimulation can have an effect on the mental body by irritating the nerves leading to pain. There are basically three types of pain that have a definite effect upon each other, and each has to be dealt with individually in order to be transformed. There is mental pain, emotional pain and physical pain.

MENTAL PAIN. The source of mental pain is negative thinking. How you think about a situation will have a definite effect on your central nervous system. This will impact the area that the thought is connected to. Therefore, if your thoughts are mentally orientated for example, much of the negative energy will impact the brain. You will feel the effects of that as mental pain. Negative thinking also has a definite effect on the emotional and physical bodies. All of these can be based on one negative thought at the same time. There is however often a hidden factor here that many miss. Let us for example say that you are in conflict with a neighbour and you decide to take violent action instead of seeking to resolve your differences through peaceful means. You may choose to physically injure that person. Physical pain is the end result of your actions. This form of thinking has become common. So where is the hidden aspect? When someone decides to make bullets and bombs, they are sold to make money. But those who create weapons are consciously aware that at some point in time they will be used to destroy lives. It is here that we find the hidden factor of mass pain being created on the physical and emotional levels.

EMOTIONAL PAIN is a common phenomenon amongst those who live their lives through their emotions. The original thought is pure, but an emotional response can overpower the mind into believing that the pain is real. Let us look at an example. A small boy is standing in the shop waiting for his mother to pay for the groceries. The boy notices a jar of sweets on the shelf and asks his mother if he can have a sweet. The mother refuses the boy's wishes because he has just finished one. The boy begins to cry and say "I want another sweet" but the mother again refuses. The boy cries even louder and holds his stomach as he feels pain appearing there. Now ask yourself, what is causing the pain – is it the sweets in the jar, or the boy's needs? This example illustrates that our responses to life's events are often controlled by our emotions and that they sometimes end up as physical pain.

PHYSICAL PAIN acts as a warning system that notifies us that something already has or is about to go wrong somewhere. It can be either on the inside such as stomach ache. Or it can be on the outside such as a burn. Pain on this level helps to avoid further injury. This aspect of pain is strongly connected to our basic survival instincts.

HOW DOES PAIN AFFECT YOU?

If you for example were to cut your arm, blood would appear and the central nervous system would create a sensation of pain to notify your mind that an injury has occurred in that area of the your body. This in turn helps to activate the correct chemistry needed to deal with it, such as stopping the bleeding. This you could say is true physical pain. Emotional pain on the other hand is created through your needs, desires and insecurities. This can be for example when you long for something that you cannot have. This is deeply connected to your reward system which continually seeks the pleasure of being rewarded, such as recognition of some kind. Physical pain can come from deep anxiety and fear as well as from stress and worry. This is a common phenomenon in today's business world. Both worry and stress factors have a deep and often long lasting effect on the central nervous system, which can create secondary effects. Stiffness in your neck or shoulders is an example of the end result of stress. All systems of pain seek to tell you that there is something out of balance in your life. In which area that is will determine the course of action required to transform the pain.

HOW DOES MY PAIN INFLUENCE MY WORK?

Any form of pain that you may have is bound to have a negative effect in some way on your work. Back ache or pain is quite a common occurrence in our working environments, which can be caused by simply having a poor quality chair to sit on. This will eventually give pain to the body. Stress and tension is often the root cause of headaches. Without rest, the pain could gradually become stronger and the only cure is complete rest and relaxation.

If you have headaches whilst at work then it is a sign that you probably are under a lot of stress. The headache prevents you from being clear, because you are not truly focused on the job when you have a headache. The answer is usually to take a pill or two to block the pain. However, after taking a pill for headaches, you may not feel the pain but it is still there. And so is the reason why you had the pain in the first place. Any form of pain limits your ability to work clearly, peacefully and harmoniously with yourself and others.

HOW DO PEOPLE WITH PAIN INFLUENCE THE WORK ENVIRONMENT?

Pain can jump from one place to another in your physical body. You can and often do hold another person's pain. But why and how does it influence the working environment? Generally speaking we all care for each other. We share our lives on the same planet, we share similar eating and drinking habits, and we all sleep, wash and dream in similar ways. So when another person is suffering in your workplace, so is everyone else, on a subtle level. But try not to hold other peoples pain for longer than is required for you to truly understand why it is happening. Otherwise you could be dragged into a situation that has nothing to do with you. Let us for example say that a colleague at work complains to you that their boss is a pain. Do you agree or disagree? If you agree, then you will have judged the boss and will have also taken in the negative energy of the person who told you. There is an energy exchange taking place here that may somehow indirectly begin to irritate you. If you hold on to the irritation, then it may appear as a pain in an area where you may have a weakness. The end result is that the irritation has caused you pain. This is secondary pain.

HOW TO TRANSFORM PAIN?

There is no quick or easy answer, but here are some important aspects for you to consider. Healing can take place as soon as you begin to take responsibility for why you have developed the pain.

- Ask yourself, am I creating my own pain or am I holding another person's energy which is creating the pain that I feel? If you feel it is your pain, on whichever level it may be, you have to start take responsibility for it. See chapters "*I take responsibility for my feelings*" and "*I understand my pain.*"

- Transform your stress factors. By deciding to take positive steps to transform your stress factors, you are learning to transform your emotions and this will help reduce the emotionally created pain. See chapter "*Stress.*"

- Use your breath to breathe positive thoughts into your pain. By learning to breathe properly you will also learn how to breathe positive energy into and through your pain. You will be surprised how effective this method is to help release pain. The opposite of this is to stay focused on the pain itself, this gives it more energy not less, and the pain will increase due to the mental activity that is being directed towards the pain. See chapter "*Breathing techniques.*"

- Transform your negative thought patterns into positive ones. One of the most positive things you can do to transform your pain is to not think negatively or to over stimulate your emotional body's responses to everyday living. Positive thought is self-healing. See chapters "*I say no to old thought patterns*" and "*Rewire your mind.*"

- Avoid, if possible, taking pain killers. On all levels of pain, we often choose to avoid the feelings of pain by taking medicines that essentially will block (not cure or heal) the pain. Whenever you do this, you are to a great degree avoiding an opportunity for a natural healing process. Very often the pain will return, even in another area, but from the same source.

Past Experience

WHAT IS PAST EXPERIENCE?

Past experiences are happenings that the body holds memories of. The memories can be linked to emotions that also are stored in the body. Our past experiences give us an understanding of the measure of time. History is a measure of time. Time can also be understood by the concepts of past, present and future. See chapter *"Time."* All of our memories are to be found within our past experiences. Past experiences are aspects of the physical time orientated system, which is meant to guide our choices and decision making.

HOW DOES PAST EXPERIENCE AFFECT YOU?

If you were to ask yourself the very basic question "where are my thoughts at this present moment?" Your answer would probably be either in the past or future. We make great use of our past experiences, because experience is the teacher of life. Those experiences, depending on whether they are positive or negative, can have a strong influence on the choices you make. It is here that you may feel fear which originates from a negative past experience that may stop you from taking a step forward. If, on the other hand, you have had a positive past experience it may take you into that next step with no hesitation in your belief that it will be the same as before. This can however lead to an addictive pattern that seeks to fulfil the pleasure and reward system. Whichever way you look at it, whenever you are not being present, then a past experience can have the effect of stopping you from experiencing the true moment and the magic that is in it. You cannot live in the past because it has already happened, just as we cannot live in the future because it has not yet happened. If you are lost in your experiences of the past you cannot fully enjoy the moment. The very moment that you are in can never return or be lived in the exact way again. Every moment has to be experienced fully in the very instant it occurs, or else it is gone. Past experiences act as mirrors that give the opportunity for change to occur, but if you fear that change due to a past experience then that moment will have been lost. You will keep attracting the same experience through your fear of it, until the fear has been transformed. This can have a strong effect on what you are doing in the present moment. You may deny or fear what is happening and then this may prevent from you taking a positive step forward.

HOW DO MY PAST EXPERIENCES INFLUENCE MY WORK?

If you have had a negative experience in the past regarding your work and you have not understood and healed it, then the energy of that experience will be held in your consciousness as a negative energy. That experience may be held in your unconscious. If you are carrying such a negative experience and someone has pushed that button, it may well reappear as a negative force. Such a negative force can be activated by a colleague at work who may unknowingly draw out that unconscious experience by saying something to you. You may become angry with a workmate for no obvious reason. It can be like a backlash of the anger that is stored away.

HOW DO OTHER PEOPLE'S PAST EXPERIENCES INFLUENCE THE WORK ENVIRONMENT?

An example could be that a colleague can carry negative experiences from their personal life into your workplace. Here again it could be released onto another person. If fear is connected to a past experience and that issue rises in your workplace, it may make you short tempered or intolerant of others. On the other hand if that person has had a positive past experience such as a great skiing weekend then they would be happy, thus spreading a happy energy in the workplace. If others around you in your working environment are holding negative experiences regarding work, then the whole working environment will also be present in the negative energies of the workplace. Such an atmosphere is not healthy for encouraging the expansion of innovative ideas amongst the workforce; in fact it does the opposite. Continued negativity will keep you focussed on the negative experience. You may become engrossed in self pity instead of being focussed on your creativity.

HOW TO TRANSFORM NEGATIVE PAST EXPERIENCE?

- You must first accept what has happened. This is necessary for the true transformation of negative past experiences to take place. Acceptance brings you into the moment. Then forgiveness can release the old in order to move on. Without acceptance the door will remain closed because you have locked yourself into that past experience. It has power over you and will seek to control your thoughts and feelings. This keeps you in the dungeon of your negative thinking, causing stress and worry that will drain the physical body of energy. See chapters "*I accept*" and "*I forgive.*"

- Learn to be present. By staying in the now you are being present in your light force. Whenever you are fully present, the past or future cannot influence you by keeping you in the drama, and you will not feel like you are the victim. See chapter "*I am present.*"

- Breathe to help release your negative past experiences. Feeling sorry or guilty for yourself are emotional responses to your insecurities which you may have experienced in the past. As an example of the transformation of such energies you can take a deep breath or several to help release those feelings of guilt or sorrow that rise from within. Breathe into what you feel is there with a positive thought. Then you can release what appears with the out-breath by giving it back to the universe for healing. See chapter "*Breathing techniques.*"

- Give back what is not yours. If you are holding past experiences, or aspects of those experiences that are not yours, then their energy can interfere with your own feelings and thoughts. This needs to be cleared out from within your emotional body and mind as soon as possible.

Projection

WHAT IS PROJECTION?

You often give out your thoughts without knowing and it may also happen that you do not take responsibility for them. Your thoughts are powerful and have an effect on all things, even if you are unaware of it. This is why it is important to guard against negative thinking as the energy from a negative thought is often passed to others. If something is happening to you and you do not take responsibility for it, then you may project your thoughts or anger to another person. This could mean that you blame that person for things happening in your life that you choose not to take responsibility for. It is also true that you project your voice in a way that reflects your feelings about the situation and to those who are present. As an example you often speak more quietly to a child than to an adult. The spoken word is a power source and it is an energy form that can have lasting effects both in positive and negative ways, depending on how you use your consciousness to express your chosen words.

HOW DOES PROJECTION AFFECT YOU?

If you blame someone about something they may have done or said, they may want to attack back. Both aspects are Ego-based. This solves nothing; it merely creates hatred and anger towards the situation or person. Anger is like food for the

Ego, the Ego identifies with anger. It gives the Ego a reason to strike back. This will have the effect of taking away the attention and energy from what you may be trying to solve, which then becomes an identity issue between the people concerned (see chapters "*Identity*" **and** "*Ego*"). It is important to deal with such an issue as soon as possible or it can grow into something much bigger.

HOW DOES MY PROJECTION INFLUENCE MY WORK?

If you are protecting yourself then you are likely to lack Self worth (see chapter "*The Self*"). If you lack Self worth you will be lacking in Self confidence, which can have a negative effect on your work by you projecting blame on others. In this situation it may be good to look at where those feelings come from. They may not be yours; you may have been told at an early age that you were not worthy or not good at anything. Then someone in your work pushed that button and you projected negative words to that person. This can create great tension between people in a workplace. The opposite is also true when you hold a healthy attitude of Self worth and being true to your Self. Then you shine and others will be influenced by your positive presence.

HOW DO PEOPLE WHO PROJECT INFLUENCE THE WORK ENVIRONMENT?

Within the corporate world, projection can be attributed to a number of areas, such as when you dictate (project) conditions and terms. You may be projecting the time when a task needs to be finished. Making a projection into the future that is based on current trends is also a common way of projection. This can be powerful as it might raise people's expectations.

If someone at work is projecting their negativity onto you, you may become lost in it if you take it personally. When you do not take things personally and give back what was projected onto you, then you will give the responsibility back. This is the mirror effect that makes it possible for that person to take responsibility for what is theirs. It will also help raise the energy in your working environment in a positive way. It is important that you are aware of how you project your thoughts, words and emotions onto others. Your thoughts will have the effect of activating action and reaction, cause and effect. If you are holding a greater sense of Self worth, then your projection power will become a strong way for you to positively influence others. Remember that your energies travel and are felt all over the world, regardless of how small or insignificant they may feel too you!

HOW TO TRANSFORM PROJECTION?

Here is some general advice to avoid projection:

- Stop judging others and yourself in negative ways.

- If someone is projecting their negative thoughts or feelings onto you, learn to send this back so that this person can take responsibility for their thoughts and actions.

- Learn to be present in all situations, then past or future projections cannot be used in negative ways. See chapter *"I am present."*

- Learn to be calm and balance your emotions. Use the space between breaths to calm down a situation that is disturbing your inner peace. See chapter *"Breathing techniques."*

- Accept what has happened, and then you will learn to embrace the moment rather than blame a situation or person. See chapter *"I accept."*

- Transform your fears and you will not be looking for faults in others. Then negative projection will not be present. See chapter *"Fear."*

Here are some basic steps to resolve any projection issues that have come up at work:

- Bring whatever it is into the present, and then past judgements become irrelevant.

- Do not focus on identity issues, such as who is the boss, this is Ego at work.

- When you are present without Ego, ask "where do we go from here?"

- By projecting your focused energies towards solving the problem and not escaping by looking for fault or altering the system that no longer works, much energy, time and resource will be saved.

Protection

WHAT IS PROTECTION?

There are two basic forms of protection that are fear-based. The first method of protection is your *natural survival instinct*. This is fixed into your consciousness to guard you against anything that you feel is dangerous. Anything that you feel may cause harm and injure the Self will start this reaction. A simple example is how we wear protective clothing in winter to prevent us from freezing. The second form of protection is fear-based. An extreme example of this is that some people have bodyguards to protect themselves from being attacked. This is how our societies have deteriorated, to the degree that the value of another person's life has become meaningless. Another example of this form of fear is when you value your material possessions highly, which creates a fear of losing them.

HOW DOES PROTECTION AFFECT YOU?

The protection you find yourself using can be far away from your healthy basic survival instincts. The fear-based protection can be caused by your insecurities. One of the strongest forms of protection is denial. An example of this can be found when you hide behind a story. You may create a drama or tell a story saying that you were the victim, instead of looking at what has happened to you and what it is trying to tell you. The story can be about you being a victim, but it is still a form of protection under disguise. If you find yourself looking outside of yourself for answers or you try to get support from someone by convincing yourself that you are a victim, then you are in fact stuck in the drama created by your Ego. In this way you often hide or escape what you do not want to see. Another form of protection is when you cover up for another person's mistakes. Why is this? To lie is another classic form of protection that often has far-reaching consequences. There is no justification for lying. It is a form of betrayal of your Self. Whenever you lie, you are stepping away from your truth and light. A lie always carries a dark side, an energy vibration which has a negative effect upon your psyche. It is a negative force that creates the mistrust which corrupts the societies we live in. It is the Ego's way of justifying its needs. A lie is always fear-based. You can sometimes lie for material gains, which are temporary needs and desires of the lower nature (the Ego). You may find yourself being carried on a wave of fear factors that are conditioning your psyche through various communication methods, such as advertising and media in general. There is an enormous energy field of fear around which whole industries have been created. These industries provide people with many forms of protection on a material level. There are a great variety of insurances, alarm systems and other types of security solutions. These are meant to protect us, but they also have the effect of eroding our intuitive qualities. It is one thing to protect based on the natural instinct and another to control and protect through fear! Over-protection is a controlling method that is frequently used to put fear into peoples' minds and hearts. As a result, much energy can be wasted or used by programming people to fear. This often results in stress.

HOW DOES MY PROTECTION INFLUENCE MY WORK?

You can become overprotective of an idea or a project that you are working on. This can have the negative effect by blocking others out. To be caught up in your work and be protective of it can cause you to not notice what is taking place around you. You may be protecting yourself from being hurt because you fear failure, and will therefore not be using your full potential in your work. You may be protecting yourself from another person or group due to their negativity or anger, for example. It can also be that you are protecting yourself from hearing the truth. You may be protecting a colleague from the boss who does not like that person. This can backfire on you if they do not settle the situation themselves because you have placed yourself between their energies. You may also protect yourself from failure by not taking on a project that you believe is risky.

HOW DO PEOPLE WHO PROTECT INFLUENCE THE WORK ENVIRONMENT?

Whenever protection is present, so is fear. So what is it that may be so fearful in your working environment which makes others protect themselves? When protection is present, openness, truth, sharing and joy is not. When all of these qualities are absent in a workforce then distrust, protection and sadness will fill the working environment. Another form of protection could be that you, your boss, or anyone else could be protecting a product or a system that they are not willing to change. This can have a negative effect by blocking innovative ideas from flourishing.

Here is some basic guidance that may be useful. Remember that all forms of protection are either instinctive (being the natural instinctive quality to protect yourself from possible harm) or are fear-based. It is the second aspect that you may need to concentrate on.

- When something does not feel right, ask yourself if you are protecting "You" from your Self. If so, why? If it is not a natural form of protection, then fear is there. Have a closer look at the fear and see what it is telling you. Be true to your fear by facing it. Ask questions like - why do I fear this person or the next step? What is it that I am protecting? See chapter *"Fear."*

- Learn to be present. This will take away the influences of past events which may be controlling you. It will also take away your worries of the future. See chapter *"I am present."*

- Do you protect others? By protecting others you may prevent them from learning a valuable lesson. Stop over-protecting others so that they can grow from their own experiences.

Rejection

WHAT IS REJECTION?

You have probably at sometime in your life experienced how it feels like to be rejected. You may have also experienced how it is to reject another person. Rejection is the act of pushing someone away – either mentally or physically. Another form of rejection can be related to your belief system. You may for example reject a religion or a political party because they no longer suit your beliefs. This is related to saying no to something. Those who are connected to the same believes that you have just said no to may then choose to reject you because of your shift in beliefs. Here, there are no winners or losers; there is the experience, because rejection is Ego-based. It chooses between one or the other. If you for example do not turn up for an agreed meeting (because you do not like the person's opinion) you are giving a strong indication of your position purely on the lower consciousness level, which means that you are actually rejecting yourself. Everything you do is mirrored back to yourself (see chapter "*The mirror effect*"). If on the other hand you were to say "I have decided not to attend your meeting because my way of thinking has changed on the subject" it becomes another form of energy because you use different words to describe your feelings and thoughts. All forms of rejection can have a strong influence on the mental and emotional energies if you are unable to accept the situation of being rejected. You can reject others purely by sending thoughts of rejection towards that person and that person will feel it in themselves. Examples can be that the physical body always rejects an implant of another organ, drugs have to be used to stabilise it. You might be rejected from entering a club if you are not following their dress code. Yet another example is that you may face criticism of a speech you gave or you may even be rejected by those who judged your performance. Rejection is Ego. It seeks to separate people from each other.

WHAT IS IT LIKE TO BE REJECTED?

Rejection comes in many forms and it might be difficult to recognise that you are being rejected. You may first think that here is something wrong with you or what you are doing. Someone may reject you because you do not believe in that person's opinion. They may have taken it personally and chosen to reject you. This is like an endless cycle that you get caught up in. All forms of rejection might lead you to questioning your truth. If so, do you choose to listen to another person's judgement of you? If you do then you may become lost in self pity because you make yourself a victim. You will be trapped in a drama created by your Ego. Whenever you take something personally you are in danger of becoming stuck in that drama or victim scenario.

HOW DOES BEING REJECTED AFFECT YOU?

Have you ever felt that you were being rejected because no one wanted to listen to you or even avoided looking at you? This can leave you with the feeling that you are not being seen or listened too. If you take that personally, you could become lost in self-pity and will have created a sense of rejection. It may have opened up an old wound from a past experience. This can have the effect of keeping you in the past which will prevent you from being fully present in your power. The feelings that arise out of being rejected can be very strong, such as anger or even revenge. You may say to yourself "you do not like me, so I do not like you." This will result in the other person feeling your rejection and vice versa. It can become an endless saga. Nothing is ever personal. It is a message, so try to read it correctly. What is it that you need to look at within you to make the change?

HOW DOES BEING REJECTED INFLUENCE MY WORK?

Any form of rejection can be demoralising and can lead to forms of depression. Rejection can take the inspiration out of your work, even to the extent where your work becomes just another day at work. You may even build up the feeling of having nothing to look forward to at work because you feel the rejection from a colleague or two. You may lack power to get things done, you may also become lethargic and say "I do not care any more", and so a "let someone else take care of it" attitude can appear. If your work is continually being rejected by your manager, seek for an open meeting to sort out any differences that may be there. There could be a simple explanation and the situation could be sorted out in minutes. You could for example be rejecting yourself because you believe that you are not good enough and that your manager therefore must reject you.

HOW DO PEOPLE WHO ARE REJECTED INFLUENCE THE WORK ENVIRONMENT?

If people reject each other or each other's results, then moral can become very low, even to the extent where communication between people stops completely. Rejection creates insecurities that can become long lasting. This will be demoralising for the group and often impacts the whole company. If a company is not clear about their intentions, then communication breaks down and the workforce may feel detached and powerless regarding decisions that are being made. This will create an underlying sense of rejection. It can be unconscious and it often leads to some form of outburst from the workforce.

HOW TO TRANSFORM REJECTION?

Eternal truth can only be held in the present moment. We never really know why people do what they do. But you can accept their point of view, even if you feel you have been rejected. How to make changes in this area is a matter of energy awareness. There are intentions behind everything you do. By learning not to take things personally you will be more focused on the intent of what is being shared and what you wish to share. Then the outcome may be very different in a positive way. Accept the situation as it has happened. By taking responsibility for your feelings you will not project them onto others in a judgemental way, such as rejecting them because they rejected you first. By accepting, you will help others to relax and they will feel that they do not have to protect themselves from you. If someone rejects you, there must be a reason for it, but what is that reason? It may not even be yours to deal with. They may be rejecting you because of something that is not clear within them. In this situation you are mirroring something back to them. It can also be that you feel their rejection as a flashback from your past experiences and that there was no intent from them to reject you. You might just have created it because that is what is happening in your life all the time. It is important to take responsibility for your feelings and level of thought, even when you feel that you are being rejected. You can, from a non-judgemental place, help heal what is taking place. Notice what is really being said and look for the true intent behind it. Here are some ways in which you can view rejection in order to help transform your logical view of its meaning into higher thoughts and action:

- Stay in the present and accept the situation. That may include the fact that you do not like the situation and that you do not like to be in this kind of situation. Embrace your feelings and what is happening. This is the starting point for your inner transformation. See chapters "*I accept*" and "*I am present.*"

- Notice what your feelings are telling you. Stay true to your feelings and take responsibility for them. See chapter "*I take responsibility for my feelings.*"

- Notice the way you react to the rejection. Do you respond in the same way? How can you respond in a way that is true to your feelings and at the same time helps calm the situation instead of escalating it? Take responsibility for your reactions and actions and if they are negative try to turn them around to become positive. See chapter "*I take responsibility for my actions.*"

- Does the experience make you remember something that has happened to you in the past? Maybe it is an old emotion that pops up because the situation is similar to what you have experienced before? Someone has just pushed one of your buttons, a positive happening has occurred for you to look at it. You have been given an opportunity to learn! See chapter "*Past experiences*" for more insight.

- Are you insecure? Does your insecurity create rejection? Work on your trust in your Self and your Self love. See chapters "*I trust*", "I love myself for who I am" and "*The Self.*"

- Notice whether you really are being rejected by the other person. You could be the escape person because the one who is rejecting you may not want to look at their own issues. Notice how the rejection occurs.

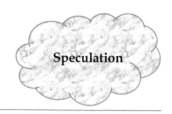

Speculation

WHAT IS SPECULATION?

Any form of speculation refers to the concept of the future and what it may hold. Speculation is based on the aspect of time, and each individual has a unique concept of time. If a person is not fully present, then their reality of the moment will not be true. It will therefore be based on their past experience and future speculation. The Stock Exchange is entirely built upon the premise of commercial or financial transactions involving futuristic speculation. With the outlook of material gains the stockbroker may advise others to invest in certain companies. Yes speculation in this way is a risky business transaction on the chance of quick or considerable profit. Speculation has its roots in the lower mind (logic). It is a behaviour patterns that contains Ego-based energy forces, such as fear and self-interest. Self-interest is the root cause of corruption. The whole insurance industry is based on speculation. This industry is also deeply connected to the fear factor. Have you ever bought a new TV, and before you left the store had the sales person ask you "would you like some extra insurance, just in case of…?" Another example of how speculative insurance works is if you have travelled by national bus or flight, you may be asked if you would like to insure your luggage. You may ask yourself whether their luggage handling is safe or not. Do you speculate on what might happen or do you trust that all will go well? Do you see it as their responsibility to handle it correctly? Do you let fear influence your decision? There are lots of questions here, all of which can create stress.

In today's financial climate one can notice how the insured, insure the insured, just in case. But as we now know, this form of consciousness has a short lifespan. Everyone on the planet has been affected by the Ego's greed and corruption of those who chose to direct their speculative consciousness in a way that even override logic itself. Is the Ego's speculative mode so powerful? The logical aspect of the mind, when combined with the Ego, is a very powerful force that constantly seeks to know what the future holds. This is because these two forces, Ego and logical speculation, find it almost impossible to be present and to live in the absolute now. To speculate is like trying to read the weather, you may get close to what may happen within a few hours or even a day, but beyond that it is impossible to have accuracy. For example the National weather forecast is very good at explaining what has happened yesterday and will also give a good forecast of today's weather. This is also relevant to the Stock exchange. You can tell what happened yesterday and today, but what comes after that? Speculation! This is why you get winners and losers back in the dualities of life, and the Ego is flourishing.

If you are always in a speculative mode when working you are placing yourself under a lot of stress. Why is this? No one person can know what the future may hold. When you are speculating you are also inviting the energy of expectation to enter your space because you are playing with the future. The pressure that is created through this lifestyle can decrease your energy due to the potential risk of failure (fear) connected to your speculation. How many times a day have other colleagues asked you to speculate? It does not have to be a big thing. It could be as simple as what is the weather going to be like tomorrow. Or you may have to increase your forecast about a new product, but what about the risk factors involved? There is always an underlying force of speculative stress, even if your forecast is conservative and your products are at the moment doing well on the market. The stress is there simply because we can never be absolutely sure about the future.

HOW DO PEOPLE WHO SPECULATE INFLUENCE THE WORK ENVIRONMENT?

In any working environment there are varying levels of speculation taking place. It could be as simple as a ground floor worker telling a colleague that what they are working on will never sell well, or even the opposite. On the other hand the person in charge of the product may be trying to sell the concept to the board with speculative future sales. Such energies – or consciousness – can have a strong influence upon the workforce. The positive speculative energy may lift the atmosphere of the working environment, which is also true of the opposite.

HOW TO TRANSFORM SPECULATION?

- Be present and you will find it easier not to speculate. See chapter "I am present."

- Try to draw everybody's attention when you are talking about something. When a person is not present, then you may speculate what their opinion is. This is because you have felt that the individual was not focused on your presentation and you do not know if they have expressed their opinion or not.

- Get acceptance for goals from all concerned. It is fine to have an ideal or a vision of some kind. It is also positive to have a common goal to work towards to produce the end result. Make sure that everyone understands and commits to the set targets.

- Being factually true and clear is a good way to prevent speculation from taking place.

- Openness with information creates less speculation as it removes uncertainty.

- Ask yourself if you trust yourself enough to trust another person. Do you also trust your intuition enough to make a decision outside of speculation?

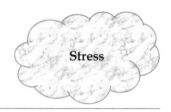

Stress

WHAT IS NEGATIVE STRESS?

Stress can be created within you when others around you are stressed and you hold their stress. Or it is self-created due to a lack of self trust in your own ability. Stress is very often connected to thoughts and worries about the future, for example with time schedules or targets to be met. It can also be connected to your own or other people's expectations of you. If you are in stress, then it means that you are not managing yourself correctly. You are not present and you are not in your true power. Stress comes from the two key areas of mental stress and emotional stress.

MENTAL STRESS: this form of stress is mainly there because you are not able to let go of your thoughts. Your logic is constantly trying to analyse and justify what is happening in all situations. The logically-based person searches for possibilities and probabilities continuously. They investigate the past and try to project that into the future to control their feelings, which is where fear is created. Much stress is unnecessarily produced in this way as there is nothing that should be analysed, and nothing to be controlled when going forward when you trust. If you have a basic lack of trust, then your mind will seek ways to justify its reasoning. By justifying yourself in this way, the Ego can step in and create fear, which eventually leads to stress.

EMOTIONAL STRESS: the emotional area in your body is a field of energy that surrounds the abdominal area. It is an extremely potent and sensitive energy field. This area picks up all vibrations and sounds within your environment and you will feel it on some level. This means that you can be affected by other people's feelings (vibrations) and sound from other sources around you. You may also be holding other people's feelings, and that can have a negative effect on your own feelings and emotions. This can be projected onto others as a form of frustration, and anger is one example of this. See also chapters *"What is stress"* and *"The Emotional Body."*

HOW DOES NEGATIVE STRESS WORK AND AFFECT US?

You often carry other people's stress. This can occur when someone, maybe a friend or colleague, approaches you with an issue or wants to share their troubles. As they hand over their trouble to you they may feel much better than when they came, but you may be holding their troubles instead. This is because they have left their negative feelings in the area of your emotional body. This is especially true if you get caught in their "drama." To be caught in another person's drama can happen if you identify yourself very strongly with their problem and maybe even take it as your responsibility to solve it. This can happen on a subconscious level as the person is unaware that they are doing this to you. Be careful when you are left with a feeling of guilt after spending time with someone. You may have picked up someone else's emotions about a situation and made it yours. Here are some aspects that can create stress:

• You have high expectations of yourself.

• You do not have enough time to do what is required.

- Other people have expectations of what should be achieved by you or how you should be or act.

- There are targets that have to be met and you worry that you will not make them.

- You judge yourself or you are being self-critical.

- Others are not fulfilling their part towards the goals set.

- You feel that you are not being heard or listened to.

- You are unable to say no to someone or something.

- You are not giving yourself time to be with you.

- You are not taking care of yourself.

HOW DOES MY STRESS INFLUENCE MY WORK?

Any stressful environment has an aura of being speedy, which is different from being busy. Being speedy takes energy from the body due to its connection to stress. It is very inefficient and takes energy when you are running around trying to catch up with something. If you are motivated then you can be busy in a harmonious way. This happens when you are true to yourself and do things that harmonise with you. You can in such cases work efficiently and this does not take energy out of the body, but feeds it instead through your creative flow. Just remember that it is good to rest in between "doing" in order to stay in that creative and positive flow.

HOW DOES OTHER PEOPLE'S NEGATIVE STRESS INFLUENCE THE WORK ENVIRONMENT?

Because stress is an irritation, it can have a negative effect in your workplace. When others in your workplace are under stress it may affect your creativity and productivity due to the tolerance level being low. Individuals may have no patience regarding issues that are work related. Joy may not be present because stress is limiting their flow. You may find yourself running around to get things done because you feel other people's stress and you are not able to communicate with them because they do not have time. In such cases you are not present, which is where things can start to go wrong.

HOW TO TRANSFORM STRESS

- One of the first steps to take is to recognise that you are stressed.

- Then you should be asking yourself; is this stress mine or is it someone else's? If it is yours, then you must try to release it. For example you can breathe deeply into the solar plexus with positive thoughts of calming that area down. This will help to release some of the tension through the out-breath. When you recognise that you may be holding and carrying other people's stress, then it must be cleared out as soon as possible. Again you can use the breath in the manner that is given above, but this time you can consciously send that feeling back to the person who gave it to you, or you can send it out into the pool of universal healing for it to be transformed. See chapter *"Breathing techniques."*

- This third step is to stop repeating stressful activities. You do this by changing your patterns. See all other chapters in the complete *"Fear and Control"* section. Read about how to transform negative aspects and you will also have transformed your stress, as this is a result of the other conditions.

The Ego

WHAT IS THE EGO?

The Ego is a form of energy that is made up entirely from the third dimensional consciousness, lower mind logic and emotions. The lower mind fears your higher consciousness. In other words the Ego is a self-made illusion that is based in the lower consciousnesses. Therefore all of our fears are self-created illusions. The vast majority of people believe their fears to be real, but they are as real as you make them. The Ego's aim is to keep you either in the past or the future, or sometimes in both at the same time. If you are seldom present then you are lost in the illusions of the past and future and are not experiencing the magic of the present moment. The Ego continually tries to make you believe that the past and future are the realities of your life. It will say to you, hold on to your fears, judge others, and keep on needing and expecting things. These are identity points from which the Ego feeds itself in order to keep the illusion alive. The Ego creates these traps to separate you from your light and truth by trying to continue to keep you in the dark.

The Ego is about identity from the outside as in other things and people. The Ego judges in order to separate you from your love. It will tell you this is pleasure, when it is pain. It will say; I like this but not that. The Ego seeks to control all aspects of your life by teaching you to fear what you cannot see or understand from a logical point of view. The Ego's identity is a shadow that steps in front of you to say that you cannot step into the present, into the light, into truth nor have faith of the Self and universe. Fear, judgement, jealousy, greed, corruption, lies, expectations and needs are some of the tools that the Ego uses to control your life:

HOW IS THE EGO CREATED?

The Ego is a state of mind and emotions. That mind is your lower consciousness (logic) that requires an identity, called "lower personality." The Ego seeks to maintain its identity through creating fear and needs at the same time. What you desire and want but often cannot have is part of the Ego's identity. It will tell you that this is pain when your soul will tell you it is joy. The Ego is created by you not being true to your Self - the Self being your higher consciousness - your light. The Ego is a shadow that seeks to control all aspects of the Self which includes your emotions, expectations and fears. The Ego becomes angry when it does not get what it wants. This could be a job, a car, a girlfriend/boyfriend, or a reward of some kind. The anger that arises is fear-based and that fear comes from an insecurity that is controlling your life in a negative way. The Ego hates any form of rejection and as such will do everything within its power not to be rejected, even at the cost of another person. This means the Ego only identifies with itself. This is how energy works and how the Ego can be created through attitudes that are negative. Jealousy is such an example. It is a strong imbalance in the emotional body through which the Ego can control you and others.

HOW DOES YOUR EGO AFFECT YOU?

One of the main effects that the Ego has over you is to keep you from being present. It achieves this in part through judgement. Judgement separates people in order to give the Ego an identity. The Ego is all about outer identity, which is chiefly found through materialism and vanity. The real Self is about who you are as a soul. If the Ego has a hold on you, it can drive you towards greater material wealth and needs. The reward is to be seen with a big new shiny car, or a new house or even a higher position at work. The rewards the Ego seeks are endless because the hole can never be filled. This can create a lot of heartache, pain, stress and sorrow in your life. The Ego is all about achieving for the sake of the identity. The Ego will take you in another direction from love and compassion. This is because there is always a price to pay for the Ego, it is extremely demanding. Payback time could be as simple as buying a new coat when you do not require one. It could be a change of car for a newer model, but after a week or so the magic you first felt when you looked at your new car in the morning will have changed, and after a month you will no longer notice it. What then? Get another new car?

HOW DOES MY EGO INFLUENCE MY WORK?

People who identify with their Ego will help another person in order to be noticed. A person who identifies with their Self will do it because their heart is there. One of the over-powering effects of the Ego is that it can make you selfish; it is all about the "I". I want this or that, or it is me who is important here, look at what I have done! This is identity seeking through achieving. If for example your baseline in work is to achieve purely for material gains, then there is no real substance to your work ethic. If your baseline in work is to be recognised, then there is no real substance to your work ethic either. In other words the Ego always seeks rewards, as its recognition is achievement. But it can be a lonely place because the reward has no substance. When you have reached a certain target set by the company or yourself, it will leave you with an empty feeling because the satisfaction is temporary.

HOW DO PEOPLE'S EGO'S INFLUENCE THE WORK ENVIRONMENT?

If you have a group of people in a working environment whose drive is Ego-based then problems will arise. Here are a few insights into how the Ego can separate a workforce:

- It will create an atmosphere of competition.

- It separates the workforce through judgement.

- When they do not get what they expect to have, the red flag goes up.

- If a large part of the organisation is Ego-based then this will prevent the majority from being intuitive and innovative. These qualities are not in the Ego's rule book.

- It will try to prevent colleagues from being present and creative.

- It does not like any form of rejection, which can be stressful for colleagues.

- Be mindful of your thoughts. Say no to the Ego and say no to old thought patterns. See chapter "*I say no to old thought patterns.*"

- Admit that you have an Ego! Then the Ego can be transformed by you simply denying it power from your lower mind and your emotions. Give yourself power through your higher thoughts. Listen to your Self. See chapter "*The Self.*"

- Do the opposite to what the Ego is trying to make you do. In this way you will also be cutting off its power.

- Look at how you respond to any given situation. This will tell you where you are within yourself. If you are in your Ego it will show itself in the following ways:
    - If you judge another person or a situation, you are in your Ego.
    - If you say that I like this and not that, you are in your Ego.
    - If your achievement is about recognition, you are in your Ego.
    - If you fear being true to yourself, you are in your Ego.
    - If you attack another person or situation, you are in your Ego.
    - If you help others in order to be seen, you are in your Ego.
    - If you are in another person's business without their permission, you are in your Ego.

As you may now be able to see, the Ego is always about me, me, me or I, I, I. Nothing else really matters to it. The Ego views the world as black or white, right or wrong. Through self study of the few examples above, you may begin to transform the Ego within.

Worry

WHAT IS WORRY?

The conditions of worry, irritation and fear are interconnected and widespread in all societies. All forms of worry are
related to future possibilities that sometimes are combined
with past experiences. Worry is a state of mind that impacts
on the emotions and creates stress. It is a mental imbalance
that pours like a stream of emotional energy into your solar
plexus. This often creates irritation that affects the whole
abdominal area. Worry is like a rocking chair that is taking
you nowhere.

HOW DOES WORRY AFFECT YOU?

Worry is related to the following:

- Time – when there is not enough time to complete something, then you may worry about not being finished on
time.

- Matter – when you feel that you need material things you
may worry that you will not get them. Or if you already
have them, then you might worry that you will lose them.

- Past – when you recognise negative things from the past
then you may worry that they may happen again.

- Future – when you do not trust yourself with the actions or direction that you are taking, then you might worry about the future.

- Someone else's feelings or "drama" – when you take on something that does not belong to you, then you may worry about that person or situation.

- Fear of making mistakes – this is an intense form of worry.

All forms of worry have underlying irritation factors, which can be felt as a lack of trust. This could for example be related to expectations that are not met, that you are not able to move forward or an inability to take decisions or positive actions.

If you worry, then your life energy is blocked. When this occurs then the physical body becomes devitalised. One basic factor behind worry is fear of making mistakes. When you live your life in this way then you are, to a great degree, living it in the past and trying to make the future safe. Fear of the unknown is a very powerful feeling to overcome. If you do not trust yourself, then it is very difficult to trust others. You also give your power away by not trusting yourself and then worrying instead. One effect of worry is that it can rise into the mental body. At this point then the fear factor can have a real hold upon your life, whereby worry can override all rational and intuitive behaviour. When it gets to this point then you are in a state of confusion and in total distrust of yourself and others around you.

HOW DOES MY WORRY INFLUENCE MY WORK?

Worry is a negative vibration that affects your whole body system. If you are worrying about something then you are irritated, and that irritation could build up over a period of time. It will seek a form of release that may come out as anger. The anger could be directed towards anyone, such as a colleague or a group. But it may have nothing to do with the person or the group as it is your own worry that has created the frustration.

HOW DOES PEOPLE'S WORRY INFLUENCE THE WORK ENVIRONMENT?

If there are a number of worried people in an environment, then tension and stress will be present. This may not be obvious at first but it will over a period of time gradually begin to show in small ways, such as someone complaining about the smallest thing. This is an outer projection and is a way of releasing the inner stress caused by worries. Those people may share their worries with you and others. How do you deal with that? If you take it in and hold it longer than a few seconds, then you might end up carrying and being responsible for another person's worry. This can be contagious. Worry spreads, and can infect a whole group of people, even a whole population.

HOW TO TRANSFORM WORRY

- Time – when you are doing things from your soul's desire to serve, then you will be given the time needed to complete what you have set out to do. It is also when you are not being present with yourself that time is an issue. Others may have expectations of when you should be ready. Set your priorities from what you feel is right and make sure to take out all other activities. You should also be patient. Maybe the time that you set as the target for finishing is not the optimal target to complete the task. Be attentive and listen and feel what comes back to you. Follow what comes your way during the journey – unexpected help may also be around the corner. See chapters *"I follow my inner compass"*, *"I am present"* and *"Time."*

- Matter – to desire and need fewer material things is one way to have less worry. To trust that what you basically require will be provided is another way of transforming your worries in this area.

- Past – it is important to transform your past negative experiences. See chapter *"Past experience."* When you have transformed them, you will no longer worry that your past experiences will repeat themselves in the future.

- Future – build on your trust. See chapters *"I trust"* and *"I decide."* When you trust yourself then you do not have to worry about what will happen in your life.

- Someone else's feelings or "drama" – make sure that you only take responsibility for what is yours, and not someone else's feelings. Give the other person's feelings and problems back as soon as possible, or transform them from within yourself. See chapter *"I take responsibility for my feelings."*

- Fear of making mistakes – trust yourself and what you are doing. See chapters *"I trust"* and *"Fear."*

REFERENCE

Reference

BEING PRESENT –
THE UNDERLYING PRINCIPLES

There are six underlying principles that are important to understand in order to obtain a balanced picture of what being present means. They are the aspects of past, present, future, time, distance and matter. These are the six main wheels which help structure our societies through logical thinking and which create the mechanistic world we live in. The six underlying principles of life are related to whatever you do. Whether you eat, drink, sleep, play, work or even breathe they all interrelate. Each principle holds an energy that affects everyone in some form. You may enter a room to attend a meeting and your presence is felt because you have physically walked into the room (your logical aspect). But you are also there in spirit, (the will 'to be') and have a third aspect of your psyche which is the presence of your soul (the heart energy). These three hold the energies of your Self together. You are basically:

- Physical body – the logical aspect.

- Spirit – the will to be, the force that moves the physical body.

- Soul – the heart energy, the love that moves all things, that guides your spirit and physical body.

Reference

If you are living your life on a logical and physical level then you are seldom fully present. This is because the Ego resides in the lower mind (logic), and there is one place where the Ego finds it difficult to be, and that is in the present. To be totally present is a momentary awareness where all eight senses are active. When touch, taste, smell, hearing and sight, with the three higher senses of clairvoyance, clairaudience and clairsentience are working together, then you have harmony. Can you be present for more than a moment or two?

BEING PRESENT

You may ask your consciousness "when am I fully present?" One thing is certain; it is neither in the past or the future. When you are present then you have access to both past and future but you are not caught up or influenced by them. This is possible because the logical mind evaluates life through the aspects of time, distance and matter. These are logical principles that relate to the concept of past and future. When you are present with children, for example, you are accessing your higher consciousness, because small children demand you to be present with them. Your higher consciousness is able to hold the past and future without being influenced by them. When you are being present you accept all things for what they are. There is no judgement involved. There is a happening and an experience taking place. It is impossible to corrupt that moment with past experiences or futuristic fears because your truth is present. You are in your light and in your power.

WHY IS IT SO DIFFICULT TO BE PRESENT?

Here is part of the problem with not being present. The Ego wants to control you by trying to make the future safe through its own ideology. But if the future has not yet happened, how is it possible to make it right? The answer is simple, it never can. If you look more deeply at your behaviour patterns, you may realise that when everything is going well for you, there seems to be a good flow to life. When all seems well in your world you do not worry or have anxious thoughts about the future. There seems to be no need for the logic to fear anything, it believes it has fixed everything, that no change can happen, and that everything will continue just as it always has. But when you do some self-study, you may find that you are actually between 15-20% fully present with your work and life in general. You may excuse yourself by saying that you have a target to reach or you may have put yourself under a lot of pressure by doing too many things at once. The stress factor can be high, but it is as real as you choose it to be. This may seem unfair, but it is within you to say "no" to stress. For example, when you are under pressure, the time factor can easily kick-in when you are trying to achieve. An unrealistic goal might have been set which from the beginning was impossible to reach. The Ego's reasoning of this is to say "it is a motivating factor and we need to push for it." But why do you need to create this stress? Some would argue that the adrenaline is needed as a motivating force. Some get caught in that adrenaline rush, and it can become addictive. Then the crash happens because the physical body can no longer maintain such pressure. What do you do then? Do you change the way you see things in order to act differently or do you take another cup of coffee to keep you going? Coffee and stress can be addictive. If you are present then your presence will be calmer, more collective and stronger. It will not set you off on a stress journey. You will not feel that you need to be busy doing things just to avoid being guilty.

If you find yourself caught up in the past or in the future then you are in the three different energy fields of the logic, emotion and Ego. It is here that the psyche can become confused by not being present. This is because the past is history, which is how time is measured through history. We know we cannot change it, so why do we spend so much time thinking that we can? There is a wise saying: "No two moments are the same." The future has not yet happened, but the mind often tries to make it so. This is because fear has been created by the Ego. This is mainly why people are afraid to take a chance on something new. In the business world, risk assessment is a big industry which boils down to one point, that of trust. If the individual or group's decision has an underlying energy of fear, then the choices made will be ruled by fear. This is then Ego based. The choice may seem to work in the short term, but in the long run it will be the opposite. This is what we are witnessing in today's economic climate where the changes are beyond human control. The intuitive right side of the brain however has an innovative base and as such can find answers to any difficulties you may be facing. This is not experienced through the negative energy of fear and control but through the positive force of trust and intuition. The solutions and decisions that are made from trust have a sustainability that is far beyond the choices made on logical grounds. From this you may find a deeper understanding of faith of your Self.

A large amount of the business world's ideology is built upon possibilities, probabilities and speculation that is futuristic. This can be changed by being present, which gives you the opportunity to decide free from the interference of fear, expectation and need. These emotions will block your natural ability to think freely, but they will not be there when you are truly present. Developing your ability to contemplate over any given situation will give you the key to obtaining deeper insights and ideas and to go beyond the logical path of reasoning. Developing your consciousness to be present will complement your work practise. You begin to be fully focussed on the job because the whole of you is being used. This will increase your efficiency on many levels, such as energy and creativity.

HOW TO BECOME PRESENT?

Learning to be present is a state of mind transformation that requires you to think not of the time zones of the past or future, but to accept what is occurring around and within you at the present moment. Innovative thinking takes you into being present. This is where innovations can blossom. The intuitive thinker is being innovative, meaning that they are working with inner insight, looking for solutions outside of the logical box that is caught up in the past or future.

Whenever you take yourself into being present, stress somehow miraculously disappears. This is simply because the factors of the past and future are no longer relevant as you are in the present, and they do not fit into the vibration of presence. By being present you are in fact in an egoless space. Contemplation and meditation are such places. Meditation allows your mind to think in other ways, such as connecting to your higher consciousness and senses. The central nervous system calms down, and this has the positive effect of calming the whole body, including the logical mind. Meditation helps calm the mind by stopping the constant chatter that takes place within the mind itself. This is achieved by you being present in the right hemisphere of the brain. You still feel the peace in all areas of the physical self. Meditation is a natural form of relaxation, but the logical aspect of the mind has stepped far away from this wisdom. It is recommended that you start to meditate or contemplate to help calm your central nervous system and centre your consciousness. By developing inner peace you will have a clearer picture and feeling of the chaos that is taking place around you. This alone will help you understand where you are within yourself and what steps you can take to be more present.

It is clear that the breath is very powerful. For more information on the breath – see chapter *"The Breath"*. To learn to manage and use the breath to empower yourself will help you to live a more relaxed and peaceful life. Here are some insights into how you can improvise and use your breath to improve your life quality:

- Be aware of how you are breathing. This is a step closer to knowing who you are. For example you may notice that your breathing is very shallow, whereby you hardly fill your lungs. This could indicate that you are not active enough and that you are unconsciously trying to save energy. This could be because your life force (the spiritual will) is low. But when something moves that, such as a fear, you may then breathe with quick and short breaths.

- Learn to hold your breath by relaxing into it. This means that you should try to enjoy the pause between each breath. You can for example practise this when you are talking to someone. Learning to pause for a moment in order to process your thoughts before continuing to speak will help your communication. This is to be mindful of how you communicate. Try to communicate in a balanced way, rather than using your emotions as the base for communication.

- Whenever someone is attacking you verbally, breathe deeply with the thought of keeping yourself in a peaceful space. When the storm has passed take another deep breath to give your reply with insight and wisdom instead of attack.

- Help transform panic attacks by breathing into the fear with peaceful thoughts attached to it. Examples of thoughts to be used can be *"I breathe peace into my fear"*, or *"I calm myself down with my peaceful breath"*.

- Take deep and intended breaths and you can move mountains. We often do this unconsciously when we sometimes take a deep breath before stepping into the unknown. The deep breath that comes with a clear and good intent can help transform pain to lesser pain. You can achieve this by simply focusing on the breath and not the pain. You then breathe a positive energy into the pain, which will give the nerve endings that are attached to the pain another message. This alone will lessen, if not stop the feeling of pain.

- Use each breath as an opportunity to serve with insight, wisdom, joy and love.

WHAT ARE DREAMS AND VISIONS?

Dreams and visions which are with us when we are asleep and awake are very important. They are a natural and essential part of our creativity. We daydream, just as we may have an intuitive vision of something. It comes regardless of how old you are!

WHERE DO DREAMS AND VISIONS COME FROM?

The mental images of your daydreaming and visions must come from somewhere; therefore they must have a greater purpose other than the concept of logical thinking that often confuses your imagination. Your visions are not confused; they are often presented to you as clear images. What are dreams and visions? There are countless books that give guidance relating to dreams and visions, but where and why do our dreams and visions appear? To seek to answer to these questions you need to firstly enter the domains of their creation in order to explore and understand their value as forms of insight and guidance through your own experiences. Dreams and visions have their roots in your various levels of consciousness. In this context, it is essential to understand that all levels of mind are centres of creative activity, and that dreams and visions follow the path through the various levels of consciousness that touch both the inner and outer realities of your life.

DREAMS AND VISIONS WHEN YOU ARE AWAKE

DAYDREAMING: is an act of mentally being somewhere other than where you actually are. An example could be that during a class you look out through a window and your thoughts are far from paying attention to the teacher. You may in this dream state wonder through some inspiring ideas or you could even be looking for solutions to a problem that is deep within. You hear the words of the teacher but you are not fully present with what is being taught. You are therefore not consciously connected. Science states that on average the mind loses focus every seven seconds. Then it has to refocus itself in order to be attentive to what is being said. In one respect it could be said that when you are daydreaming you are not logically connected to rational thinking. An insight into this is that when you are daydreaming you are more deeply connected to pictorial forms as the mind has stepped past logic and has entered a state of altered perception. Daydreaming on this level is not an escape from life. It may be the opposite, such as looking for insight into your creativity.

VISIONS: do you have a vision in life? Have you asked yourself where you are heading in life or what you would like to develop most? Visions are great motivators as long as they are not entirely based upon achieving, which can lead you back into the path of the Ego's needs. This is an important distinction to make. If the vision and achieving is dominated by the Ego then the path may not be so smooth. In one respect it could be said that the daydreaming comes before the vision because the vision is closer (in energy terms) to the spiritual will. In other words if you have a vision and are keen on developing it, you will find a way to create it. But the important issue here is not the vision itself; it is the intention behind it. Dreams and visions are very much connected to our creative and innovative qualities, and life without them would feel very empty. Dreams and visions on this level must therefore play an integral part in our lives. For example the very word "vision" has many connotations, here are a few:

- Unusual competence in discernment or perception; intelligent foresight.

- A mental image produced by the imagination.

- The mystical experience of seeing, with your own eyes, the supernatural or a supernatural being.

DREAMS IN THE SLEEP STATE

You could say that a dream is a line of thoughts and images that you see during the sleep state. The sleep state is a time when the soul can leave the physical body without the physical body fully recognising that the life force has temporarily stepped out from its presence. Sometimes when an individual has built many fears around their life, they often cannot sleep deeply or they have very little sleep. This is mainly stress related. They do not trust themselves either logically or emotionally, or both, and are unwilling to let go of being conscious in order to fall into the unconscious state that sleep offers. In other words they fear surrender to themselves.

Dreams are often thought to be only imaginary or are seen as a cry for help by those that pay little attention to them. Let us first explore the various aspects of dreams and their source of creation. Whenever you are dreaming you are in fact relating to at least two other levels of consciousness at the same time, which are connecting simultaneously. These are the lower and higher minds – that of 3D and 4D. Every time you fall asleep, the body and mind has a time to rest and restore. This is actually a major reason for you sleeping. The sleep state allows the higher consciousness to return to its original source whilst the physical body and the lower mind between them have surrendered to the sleep state. You sometimes sleep deeply and sometimes lightly, but there is a duality of energy that continues to work. The soul is neither in nor out of the body when you dream during sleep. It is in a kind of no man's land, which is a space that is in between realms of consciousness. This is the reason why we can sometimes remember a dream and sometimes not. Whenever we can recall a dream it means that we were more in the body and lower mind than in the higher mind. Whenever this occurs the recollection of the dream is always more complete due to it having reached a part of the brain that is closer to the lower consciousness. But even then it is rare that a dream can be fully remembered or recalled.

Some dreams have fears attached to them, whilst others do not. Those dreams that seem to bring a warning or a message of danger often relate to fears that have been put away in our subconscious. Such fears are often unable to rise through the normal channels for a variety of reasons. We tend to hide most fears from others as they may be seen as a weakness. There are indeed deep feelings involved mainly due to the controlling factors of the logical mind and the emotional body that are, for whatever reason, avoiding the message. This is why we often dream of such fears. In this sense such dreams are a positive happening as they seek to release you from the old and in this way they are not warning messages. Whenever the physical body and lower mind are not fully present there is an opportunity for the higher mind and soul consciousness to work through into the lower mind to release those blocked energies. This is what is happening many times during your sleep state. It is often the case that the lower mind uses the sleep state as an opportunity to clear out any material that is no longer required. You can in this respect see sleep as cleaning of the hard drive of your computer. This is often felt as a confused dream, which can be a dream that returns many times.

On a daily basis you receive thousands and thousands of impressions. But what is it that decides what is worth keeping? An example here could be when you are trying to recall something that you are not fully aware of. You might remember the basic information, but when it comes to re-membering the specifics about this moment you are often unable to because the information maybe held deep in the unconscious. Such events are often connected to our dreams; this is partly why you dream. It is an opportunity to recall what you may have missed because it was stored deep in the unconscious.

Some dreams occur to clear out non-essential information. Or they can come as a form of guidance, be it positive or negative. The non-essential information that is being proc-essed by our dreams usually appears as confused pictures in the mind. They may seem to make no sense and pass by quickly. This is due to the mind clearing out information that the logic deems to be of no value. This can for example occur when you are driving down the street and your eyes and mind are focused on key points, such as other cars passing or traffic lights. The rest is peripheral vision that the mind pays little attention to, as it is deemed non-essential. There might sometimes be a piece of information in the periphery that gets lost as the logic deems it to be of no importance. The higher mind knows this and the information can be processed whilst we are in the dream state, to reappear as dreams with a message. For example, you may be going through a difficult time and have issues to deal with and want to find solutions.

You may exhaust your thinking as you try to find relevant answers. When you are dreaming, the unconscious is still at work, and often comes up with another way to solve the problem. This is usually released to the logic in the form of pictures and words. When waking up, we often miss the opportunity to learn from the messages we receive because dreams are seldom written down.

Dreams often appear in symbolic form where guidance can be interpreted. The symbol can for example be an animal or a person. Study your dreams; they have a place on your spiritual path. But it is wise, as in other practices, to not become too dependent on your dreams as a tool of guidance and absolute truth. The lower mind can confuse your thoughts about the dreams if you hold fears. The logical person often thinks of the worst scenario if a dream appears to be negative when in fact it may be about rebirth instead. Death is an essential step to rebirth. This is where fears may take a hold on you, and if the dream is misinterpreted and acted upon then you could be heading the wrong way. Dreams are never absolute truth because there is room for interpretation error.

VISIONS WHILST ASLEEP

It is important to recognise that visions are on a different level of consciousness than dreams. They appear to encourage you to really listen because they provide you with insights from a higher level of consciousness. Visions are often experienced as pictures of great beauty and deep learning; they are made up of mental pictures and images that are often interpreted as mystical experiences. But where do these pictures come from and why? Visions are created through your higher consciousness. They are therefore free from the influences of the lower mind. Visions are also felt as a deeper experience of unconscious thought, bringing guidance from your higher

Self. Visions are seen and experienced through the spiritual eye, which is deeply connected to the guiding source of the universe, the perfect provider. When a vision appears to you it deeply touches your psyche. Your psyche is connected to your inner-vision but you often feel it in your body as this is where you are anchored. Such visions can be extremely profound and can have a long lasting effect on your life. They often confirm an experience you may have had, even from a past life. Due to their sacredness it is sometimes wise not to share a vision with someone else as this may take away the meaning for you. This is also true for many aspects of life; as what, why and how much you share with others in life is important to understand. This is not about fear; it is a matter of feeling and trusting yourself. If it seems right to share, then it must be so.

Visions also come in differing forms. The more direct visions come like a blast of fresh air into your life. This sometimes has the effect of waking you up to a reality that was not even thought of or experienced by you before. Such information may not have been accessible through normal channels of consciousness. Visions can take you on a journey, even back into a past lifetime which may help clear up some confusion that remains around a particular period that is blocking your progress in this lifetime. Visions can also be connected with the present, giving direction and meaning to the next steps that you may take. Or they can relate to an event that is yet to come. This is said with great caution, for futuristic work requires great respect and understanding. One such form of a futuristic vision that is often hidden in the subconscious is déjà-vu. This means "experienced before" and is a deep-seated secret of the spirit and soul. The experience is not shown to the logical mind until the moment it arrives and is meant to be seen. Then for a few moments the lower mind is confused, as it finds something familiar about something or a place that it has no previous logical memory of. The mind is unable to put this together as a true experience or meaning. The reason why the lower mind is unable to understand it is because the essence of the message in not something that the lower mind can comprehend. It is an essence that is understood by the higher mind. In one way it could be said that the future is already there, and is prepared for us! The whole meaning of this experience is to say to you that you are in the right place at the right time, and to keep on going that way. It is a signpost from the spirit to you, this is its essence of magic, trust it!

Another form of vision that we often receive is that which is consciously created through such practices as creative meditation. In this instance we are fully awake and aware of what is occurring in order to direct our thoughts towards seeking higher guidance. During such meditations, the vision appears through the spiritual eye. This is the only channel that allows a vision to be seen. The difference between the vision whilst sleeping and that of meditation is that during the practice of meditation you are fully conscious on all levels, and all levels of consciousness are being used in an effort to manifest insights in order to seek wisdom and knowledge. This is conscious growth. The practice of creative visualisation meditation is the perfect balance that will help all seekers of truth. You should always be fully conscious during meditation, as this enables the information and guidance that you receive to be stored in the higher mind, which also filters into the lower mind as a real experience, to enable you to remember it and recall it through your memory. The use of directed thought through the higher mind principle allows the meditator to access their inner wisdom. It is through the natural stimulation of the higher mind that you are able to release the holding force of the lower mind. This will lift your consciousness as a meditator. You do this through right thought, right action, right intention and the results of the experience can be very beautiful! The spirit will only meet what is pure within you; it is from here that the light can spread throughout you. When drugs are used to meditate there are great dangers involved for the meditator. Whenever you are under the influence of drugs it is like driving a ship through the fog, where your vision is clouded. What you experience is not held in the higher mind due to the fact that it was not created from a balanced consciousness. This means that the experience is not clear and is a creation of the lower mind as well as being emotionally based. The individual who is influenced by such drugs is also unable to re-visit the vision or state of consciousness in order to access the experience on that level. The person will have to take another trip, using the drug in an effort to recreate the experience. The experience will not be the same next time. This is because the control and discipline of the higher mind has not been activated through the right method and intent. In such situations only the lower mind and often the emotional body are at work. This can cause emotional energy and the anger held within to be expressed fully. Anger is often hidden behind the calming effect of the drug. Escape may also be the very reason why the person is taking the drug. The dangers of this form of escape are many. Such an individual can often be seen to be running away from their own inner power. This can leave them open to outer negative influences.

Seek your liberation through clarity of body, mind and spirit. Under such consciousness life will appear in many beautiful forms for you, and dreams and visions will be created from your truth.

ENERGY

WHAT IS ENERGY?

Energy is everywhere – it is in all aspects of life. Energy can be felt in physical ways – such as through your five physical senses (smell, touch, taste, sight and hearing), and also by the quality of the spiritual aspects – such as your intuition. Most of the energy that is around and within you cannot be seen by the physical eye. Quantum physics and metaphysics explain these energies from a scientific point of view.

HOW DO ENERGIES IMPACT A WORKING ENVIRONMENT?

The way energy works through you is no different, whether you are in your workplace or at home, it is everywhere and in all forms. How you and your colleagues manage energy or are aware of how it works will to a greater or lesser degree determine the atmosphere that is present, and what you attract into your life in the form of experiences. For example, if you have a negative thinker in a meeting, then this person can have a negative effect on those who are present. This is true even if the person's negativity is not connected to what the meeting is about. The individual could have a personal problem which they have allowed to enter the workplace. Or the individual is not stimulated in a positive manner and would prefer not to be there. That person may not be present in the meeting from an energy point of view and their thoughts might be projected towards the weekend golf game instead. Such a presence will impact the group in a negative manner, even if some may choose to ignore the behaviour. An aura is an invisible energy field that surrounds a person, and which fills the atmosphere with its vibration. All living things have an aura, from trees to animals to humans. The energy of a building and its aura is created by its location, design, and the contents within the design, such as furniture and appliances. The inner and outer colour scheme is important, as is the consciousness of those who live and work in the property. The science of Feng Shui demonstrates this in a good way. A business has an atmosphere of energy surrounding it, and whether this is positive or negative (or both) will be determined primarily by the thoughts and actions of the people within that business. If the actual intention within the business is a creative positive energy, then the building will hold that energy and all those working within that environment will feel the positive force. When you strive to create a positive workforce, the energy within that working place will touch many aspects and it will be everywhere. It will be passed along to the staff and it will be present in the board meetings. It will be in the food you eat in the canteen and it will even be in the products that are created.

When thoughts are positive, then the product will also carry a positive charge of energy. This charge will be felt by those who handle it as well as those who buy it. Let us look at an example of how energy works in the last point. There are similar products on display in a supermarket shelf or in a parts department, and an individual does not know which one to choose. That person will subconsciously pick up on the energy and is more likely to choose the product with the positive energy. This is how effective and far-reaching a positive force can be to others. Energy holds either a positive or a negative charge, but it can also be neutral. Which of these would you prefer to be in? It is your choice. You can help create a friendly, harmonious workplace simply by being positive yourself, even if those around you may seem to be the opposite most of the time. If you are able to hold your energies in a positive manner, this will affect those around you, and from there the positive force can grow quickly and influence others.

HOW DO ENERGIES WORK?

On the physical level, energies are found to be active in the mineral, plant, animal and human kingdoms. For example, crystals are used in many electrical appliances, such as computers and watches. Plants give us their energy as we eat them. This is also true for animals. Another example of how the mineral, plant and animal kingdoms share their energy with us is through the eye to visualise their presence and energy. This aspect also feeds the soul. We also hear nature, whether it is it running water or birds singing. These are all energy forms and as such have a purpose and are interconnected. We would not have fire if there was no oxygen, and we can see one of these energies, but not the other. You may feel the wind even if you cannot see it other than from a secondary point of view, for example through the passing clouds or when the leaves are moved by the wind. These are simple examples of how nature tells us how fortunate we are to experience these energy forms.

The world has an electric energy field that helps to stabilise nature itself, such as the weather. There are many forms of energy – both positive and negative - that are found in nature. Magnetic energy forms, such as vortexes and lay lines can negatively or positively affect the energy in your house and those who live within. Most Churches are built on sacred sites that our ancestors worshiped due to the magnetism of the earth in that location. It is likely that such magnetism comes from a crystal bed in the ground. Stonehenge is a place with very strong magnetism from a crystal bed, lay lines and the vibrations of the stones themselves.

THE POWER OF THOUGHT

Your thoughts are the most powerful energies you have. Thought is an energy that can travel anywhere. Your thoughts have no boundaries and you are free to think. The energy of thought is like an electrical charge that finds a target. What the target is and what the thought contains depends on the intention of the thinker. If for example you send a thought of acceptance to a colleague then that person will feel it, even if they are at the other end of the factory or in another country. The same will occur if a thought is directed to another person as a negative energy, that person or group will feel the vibration of your negative thought. Everything you see around you has been created by an original thought. That thought motivated the individual into a creative process. The thought turned into words that were followed by action. This could fit any creative or destructive process because the consciousness itself carries the original creative energy behind it.

Another way to explain thought energy is to understand that thought goes before you. Thought travels ahead of you to create what you have asked for. This is why we often find ourselves repeating or having similar experiences time after time. Your thoughts have gone to where they were directed. For example if you had a negative thought about a project or something that you have been asked to do, that thought energy will have placed itself in the area concerned and will hold that negative vibration. Those who work with it will on some level feel the negative energy. This might explain

why you sometimes feel a negative feeling about something
even before you have started.

FEAR AND HOPE

The concepts of "Fear and Hope" are deeply ingrained in the lower consciousness of individuals and are used by many. The lower mind is conditioned to believe that fear and hope are an important part of our existence and experiences. Those who are unaware of the true meaning of fear and hope, often fall into the trap of using them to either justify something or to control others. The use of these two words is often hidden behind an agenda of mistrust and as such carries negative energy. The concepts of fear and hope are deeply rooted in our cultural belief system and can be associated with a person's control issues. Fear and hope are only held in the perception of logic that is connected to probabilities of past, present and future. But for now let us focus on the past and future in order to give some deeper insights into the role that fear and hope may play in your life.

Fear is the old energy of third dimensional consciousness that has served people well in the past. It is deeply connected to the natural instinct of survival and it could be said that fear is our biggest controlling factor. Fear prevents people from ascending into the next level of spiritual development, that of higher consciousness transformation. The vibration of higher consciousness begins from the fourth dimension upwards. The illusions that fear creates prevent, in a variety of ways, an individual from accessing their higher consciousness towards greater wisdom. Your intuition is an important aspect of your psyche that is being blocked by fear.

The societies of today are becoming more dependent on gadgets or electrical appliances that on the outside seem to take care of things. The intuitive aspect is being used less and less. This is causing the deeper sense of intuition and trust to be eroded. The cell phone is used to call someone when you are five minutes late to say "I am on my way" or "I am at so and so, I will be with you soon." This is because you do not trust the Self enough to say "everything is ok." You do not trust that the universe will take care of things. Try to intuitively feel where that person may be, on a deeper level.

WHAT IS FEAR IN RELATION TO HOPE?

Let us look at an example that is used in many life situations by those who wish to control you. The person seeking to control will present you with fear. Let us for example say that this individual states that there is a planet heading towards Earth way which is going to smash into us, creating an Armageddon. On the other hand they will offer you hope by saying "buy my book – it offers you the only Hope to avoid annihilation." Many buy into this dark sales technique. Fear is a conditioning of the lower mind that tries to make you believe that your fears are real. The fearful thought empowers the fear itself. In this respect the fearful thought goes before you. This is how you continue to re-manifest your fears. This is a deep conditioning of your psyche that is very far from your truth. The truth is that people have been taught to believe that the illusion of fear is real. This is partly why fear stirs up emotional energies. This is possible mainly because your thought patterns have been conditioned. You imagine that those feelings are much bigger than what they actually are. One feeds the other. In other words, an imbalanced emotional body escalates the illusion of fear. Fear often freezes your energies. When it does this, it often impacts both your emotions and mind. For example, if you allow a fearful thought to enter your emotional body, then the fear becomes emotionally orientated rather than mental. You can in this respect become an emotional thinker. The person trying to make you feel fear knows this either consciously or subconsciously. You can become angry when the energy of fear reaches this point. The fear is purely a form of protecting the Ego. The Ego does not want to lose its identity and will do absolutely anything to keep it. This is why fear always looks outside of a person for all answers, and it needs to be fed! It is obvious that all fears are based on past events, and your experience of them determines their depth or the hold they have on you. Some may not even be from this lifetime. You often carry past-life fears into this lifetime so that you can transform them. This may explain why you keep repeating things. When you transform your fears within, then you will take yourself into a greater sense of love and universal trust. This is because Love is a higher vibration than that of fear or hope. Fear and hope cannot reside in the body or mind of a person who is fully present and loving.

The most important step to take to transform fear is to learn to be present. Then your past experiences cannot have a grip on you and you also do not waste energy on worry (fear) of the future. When you are present then you are able to accept and eventually also able to forgive. Acceptance is a key to forgiveness, and both help transform your old consciousness.

IF YOU ARE NOT TRULY PRESENT, THEN WHERE ARE YOU?

If you ask yourself at any given moment: "Where am I now - in the past or future" Quite often you find yourself in both at the same time. If this is the case, then you are not grounded in the present. Whenever you are not fully present, then the Ego is active and you are under its influence. The Ego is the seedbed of fear and hope. It is true to say that you cannot heal or transform fear with fear, or emotions with emotions. They are of a similar vibration, that of third dimensional consciousness. Fear and love cannot co-exist. When you are able to love from your heart then you are present and you will have no fear. By gradually replacing your fears with a greater sense of trust you will naturally become deeply connected to your inner-self. You will enter a higher vibration of trusting your Self. When you accomplish this you will find that you will also trust others more. You will develop an inner trust that will take you into a higher vibration. It is a knowing, call it intuition, and when you are there then the word hope becomes meaningless. You trust and you have faith.

The Ego's presence is either in the past or in the future at any given moment. It cannot, nor does it want to be, in the present moment. This is partly why the logic is always so busy in achieving things. It wants more of this or that, to make it better than this or that. But if you ask yourself what happens when you have what you want; what then, do you want more of it? There is a kind of madness in our society that is so much into achieving, that we often forget about ourselves, to be present and to be still. The Ego is always analysing and forming judgements of itself and others, this is an important part of its self-recognition and justification process. Judgement is the Ego's way of justifying itself. It says "I like this, I don't like that." This is the Ego's way of doing things which creates fears. Fears are its life force, and the lower nature is happy to keep feeding it.

INSIGHT INTO THE MEANING OF HOPE

Your fears also want to control the future as you wish it to be, and sometimes at a cost to others or even yourself. This is partly why fear and the Ego are so fascinated with the future. This is where "hope" comes into the picture. The word "hope" is often used as a way to try and justify the future. An example could be if you say to someone "I hope it will all work out well for you?" This kind of sentence always ends with a question mark. This is because no one knows what the future may actually bring. So why put your energy into hope? When you say to someone who is leaving your home: "I hope your journey will be a good one?" This leaves the question "do they know something that I don't?" Try changing it to "I trust your journey home will be good!"

Much of the insurance industry is built upon fear, past happenings and probabilities. The stock market is based upon future speculation, the unknown. But neither of these is actually in the present. So what value do they have other than material gain? Is society protecting itself based on probabilities? It seems to be that way. Whenever you do not trust yourself, you step out of your inner faith and into hope in order to fill that empty space, but with what? Is anything certain? Essentially you are distrusting yourself and are giving your power away to hoping for something better. It is the lower consciousness that has created the illusions of hope, because the Ego wants you to stay in that state of lower mind and emotional confusion of not trusting. Ask yourself, how many times you have asked another person that you hope they will "do something about it." Can you see how this puts them on the spot? Is it not about your own expectations of another, simply because you do not trust yourself? How many times have you told someone that you hope that this or that will turn out well? This is again an example of a lack of trust. At the root of this fear, there is a great force that is trying to tell you to get up and do something about it, rather than giving your power away to hope and fear. It is in this context wise to understand that your consciousness goes before you. If you have a fear, you will attract it. It appears in order to give you an opportunity to transform it, it is a gift. To turn on the light in the room where you have fear is to see where the problem may be. This is a big step towards the release of your Ego. Light transforms darkness. Darkness cannot shadow what is already in the light. Fear and hope are the tools of the Ego that seek to keep your psyche in darkness. There is no need to fear and hope for anything. They are the jail masters of the Soul. Whenever you are in fear, you are not in the love vibration. Whenever you are hoping for something, you are not present in trusting your Self.

Through your spiritual development you will be stepping into and maintaining your awareness of the higher vibration of your fourth dimensional consciousness. From there your fears and hopes will be transformed. This is a part of the greater plan of universal consciousness transformation: to clear out the old consciousness that no longer serves you.

By transforming your fears, you will no longer need the word hope in your vocabulary. You will have taken great steps towards freeing yourself from the Ego!

The discipline of meditation teaches you how to develop clear, positive thoughts. It also teaches you how to hold your inner stillness. This will help raise your soul awareness which is a step towards higher consciousness. Meditation helps you develop your higher Self (that of the soul). The old principles and ideas that come from the lower personality (the Ego) will begin to transform.

HOW CAN YOU ACCESS THE HIGHER SELF?

You must first seek your inner silence by learning to be still. Meditation teaches you this by helping your mind to think in another way. Without developing the quality of stillness you will not be able to touch your higher consciousness. When a depth of inner silence has been achieved then it is possible to enter the inner chambers of your mind. But in order to do this you must first learn to master your lower mind. Calm the mind down by focussing on peace, for example, and draw that into yourself by using your breath. The lower mind has had a whole lifetime of controlling you. When you use the method of "creative visualisation meditation" then you are giving yourself an opportunity to open up your higher consciousness. This allows you to see how you have thought before. Your dedication and self-discipline taking control of your Self will affect your life. You will begin to change old thought patterns. See also chapter *"Rewiring your mind"*.

Reference

You should always be prepared to ask your inner Self questions when you meditate so that you can get explanations in relation to what you see or are experiencing during the meditation. It is not possible to receive from spirit without asking. You have the right to seek guidance and wisdom on your journey.

SIMPLE MEDITATIONS

A simple meditation can take between 5 and 20 minutes. This meditation will help you quiet your emotions and feelings:

1. Find a quiet place to be.

2. Sit upright on a chair or on the floor.

3. Close your eyes and mentally focus on your feelings and emotions. Feel what is there and ask for it to be still.

4. Take a deep breath through your mouth into the solar plexus whilst holding the thought of stillness. Fill your solar plexus with this breath. Then hold it for a moment.

5. Release the breath and as you breathe out feel as if you are carrying any stress or tension out with the out-breath. Send those feelings out into the universal consciousness for healing (do not leave them in the room).

6. Come back to your stillness.
   Repeat this process until the emotions and feelings are calm.

You can use these six steps to calm your mind and emotions:

1. Find a quiet place to be.

2. Sit upright on a chair or on the floor.

3. Close your eyes and mentally focus on your mind. Feel what is there and ask for it to be still.

4. Take a deep breath through your mouth into the lungs and heart whilst holding the thought of stillness of your mind. Fill your chest with this breath. Then hold it for a moment.

5. Release the breath and as you breathe out feel as if you are carrying any stress or tension out together with the out-breath. Send those feelings out into the universal consciousness for healing (do not leave them in the room).

6. Come back to your stillness.

   Repeat this until a greater sense of peace within yourself is reached.

ADVANCED MEDITATION – THE CREATIVE VISUALISATION MEDITATION METHOD

There are three basic steps to follow when working with a creative visualisation meditation. Following these three steps will help you to enter your higher consciousness with clarity of what is taking place within your meditation. They are imagination, creation and perception.

Use the simple meditation to quiet yourself before stepping into this more advanced meditation.

STEP 1 – TO IMAGINE

Our imagination is deeply connected to the logical mind. Opening your imagination for this method of meditation is the first step upwards. If someone says to you "Imagine yourself standing on a beach", the lower mind will automatically take you there. This is because you have at some point during this lifetime been on a beach and therefore the mind and its imagination feels safe there. Therefore it is recreating the beach in your mind's eye again for you. It is a memory recall from your unconscious. The logical mind has had a very strong controlling factor over your life prior to you starting to meditate. This is what all developing meditation students need to master by learning to quieten the mind. The logic, which resides in the left hemisphere of your brain, is sceptical to this other side of you. It will create fear as a form of protection to try and stop you from meditating because it does not trust what it cannot see or feel, other than through the five lower senses. In creative visualisation meditation the mind is used as a tool to climb up into a higher state of mind. This is achieved through taking control over its influences by telling it to accept and trust what is being experienced by you in your meditation. It is of vital importance to calm the logic before you can move forward in meditation. You will otherwise have a constant flow of lower-thought vibrations that interfere with the pure meditation channel.

STEP 2 – TO CREATE

You can now from the first level of imagination step up into the level to create what you are visualising – the beach. The creation of what you are guided to see in a meditation is an image that is as real as the present moment. This is because you are stepping out of earth-time. You are from this state of mind crossing over the bridge from the left into the right hemisphere of the brain, from logic to higher mind. This takes you into the "all trusting" intuition. The right side of the brain does not respond to the influences of time and distance. It is a place where the logic no longer has an influence upon your physical life form. Your creative thoughts have become astral in their projection, whereby those aspects of time and distance have no bearing on you. This will then lead you to the third step, that of perception.

STEP 3 – TO PERCEIVE

This third step, to perceive, takes you deeper into your higher consciousness. It also enables you to use your higher senses of Clairvoyance and Clairaudience. Your perception on this level will give you the opportunity to study what you are witnessing during the meditation and it will be free from the control of the lower mind. You trust your journey through your presence in a higher state of consciousness and you are able to move on into other experiences. This is the point where the logical mind no longer has a hold upon your thoughts. Such flow allows new experiences to appear when universal guidance is being presented to you. It is on this level of consciousness that you will find that you are the most liberated human being.

You are now two steps above the logical mind and its influences. It is from this third level of meditation that you are able to experience the depth of your inner stillness. Here the greater awareness of the higher planes of consciousness can be grounded and explored into all levels of your consciousness. This is only possible when there is no interference of any kind from the lower planes, such as logic and emotion.

If you are not guided by a teacher or listening to a recording during such meditations, the time of return is governed by your soul. This form of meditation is the most natural way for you to develop a greater sense of peace and harmony wherever you are. Remember that when you have finished the meditation, make sure that you ground yourself properly by bringing yourself fully back into the physical body. Do not open your eyes until you feel that you have completely returned within the dense physical body.

WHY ARE YOUR INTENTIONS SO IMPORTANT?

When your intention is true then it carries the light and the power that comes with it. Your integrity will shine through. Love, peace and joy will reside in your heart and mind. Nothing will seem too big to handle, nothing too small to ignore. You will be present to explore and expand on your creativity to serve others, regardless of how they may judge you. You will know who you are and trust your vision with a faith in your Self.

WHAT IS INTENTION?

With any choice or decision that you make there has to be an intention behind it. Intention is a mental energy. It determines what course of action you may take in any given situation. There is intent behind everything you think and do. The intention could be either a positive or negative response depending upon your priorities or mindset. Your intentions can have a purpose, goal and an objective that direct which line of action you want to take.

- PURPOSE: is a key factor and the driving force behind the intention. You could call this a determination to do. For example, if you are determined to develop a new prod-

Reference

uct, then your purpose may be to develop a product that improves the customers' life.

- GOAL: this could be related to the purpose of the new product and how long it may take to reach the end result.

- OBJECTIVE: this describes what the end effect is. This result can be satisfied customers and therefore higher sales and improved revenues.

Your consciousness will, when the right intentions are behind it, give a purpose and strength to an innovative idea or a vision. There is an immense resource behind the right intent and a positive thought. If your intentions have ulterior motives then the intention behind what you do is not true to the cause. Your intentions can be Ego-based and you may lie in order not to reveal something. Another example is that your ulterior motives could be financial, and as such your intentions may make you avoid your true responsibility for the project. This usually comes at a cost to others.

WHAT ARE YOUR DRIVING FORCES?

- Is it your intention to achieve as much as possible in a short period of time?

  This aspect towards achieving is very much about making things happen. Within any individual there can be an underlying driving force to achieve. The motivation to achieve can come from a number of places. For example you may need to keep busy to avoid an inner issue that you may find difficult to transform. Or you may be a strong achiever in order to be noticed, which is being egocentric. There can also be a strong emotional presence in your achievement, such as wanting others to praise you for how good you are, for doing so much in such a short time. This is connected to a reward system, which often comes from a lack of Self worth.

- Is there an intention to avoid a given situation?

  This can be about good or bad intent. For example, imagine that you have made an error in a project, and in the following days you are obliged to face the music and give an explanation. You may become sick – an unconscious happening – to avoid that meeting or you may ask a colleague to represent you instead. In another situation you may avoid being rewarded because you do want any fuss made over what you may have accomplished, and as such your intention is to avoid such a meeting and try to escape from it.

- Is your intention to relax and move through what may be expected of you in a way that does not create stress?

  If your intention is clear and you are in your power then you feel strong and are true to your vision. The intent will also carry that positive energy. What is expected of you becomes secondary. You are being present and focused on your work and you have faith in what you are doing. You will find that those around you will also be uplifted by your positive attitude. You will be doing while being!

You may have had an experience where you felt that something was coming, such as a phone call or a letter of some kind. When it arrived, then your thought may be "oh, I knew you were going to call me or I felt that there was something coming in the post." Well yes, this could be a fair interpretation of an intuitive happening. So where does such an energy come from? Energy is everywhere, but our thoughts are the most powerful. They are the builders of the cultural societies we live in, as well as the active energies we hold. Thoughts are transient, as are your feelings. When feelings get attached to your thoughts they can travel with the consciousness to wherever they are directed. Here is an example; if you send a loving thought to a friend, who is half way around the world, your friend will feel it as if you were standing next to him. Your friend would have intuitively picked it up through the global electrical field of consciousness. Each individual is wired into this field of energy. In this way everyone on the planet is connected to each other.

The energy and vibration of your intuition is of higher consciousness. Light is consciousness. That is why it travels at a slightly faster speed than physical light and normal logical thinking. This can be easily understood if you think about a situation where you intuitively moved to avoid an object hitting you. You do it without seeing it coming. What made you move a fraction of a second before it hit you? You can be sure that it was your intuition that saved you from being hit.

Reference

Some say "trust your gut feelings," which is partly true. Your feelings are usually right, certainly the first one. Your feelings are a very good way to get to understand your intuition. The best way to capture intuition is when you have a feeling that goes before you have a logical thought about the feeling. This is your intuition at work. The feeling went straight to the right intuitive side of the brain and not to the left logical side. The intuitive thought has avoided being analysed by the logic. When the left side of the brain interferes, then you can easily have doubt, which can lead to confusion. If you do not grasp the intuitive thought at the moment it arises, then it will be gone and the logic, Ego, or both may kick in and you are lost again.

To trust your intuition, to be present and stay with it, means to trust that your first feeling and thought that came with it were right. Try to hold and follow it. The training is about learning to listen beyond normal thought patterns (which can hold fears) in order to find answers and solutions to seemingly difficult situations. One way to do this is to con-template the situation or a problem you may be dealing with. Contemplation will help lift your consciousness above logic to take you towards the intuitive. From there an insight may appear and a solution may be found. In this way you will be tuning yourself into the collective higher consciousness which does not carry the vibration of fear. Old thought patterns condition you to fear, preventing you from taking steps into the unknown. Those who choose the opposite, the logical thinking, tend to follow the crowd. Here there is a danger of becoming lost like sheep with no real leader. The Ego often seeks comfort through feelings of belonging to the crowd. It inherently dislikes any form of change. The Ego wants to stay with the old because it has worked so well for so long. It is the typical, logical way of thinking. The logical thinking will often correctly say, as it did in 1900's, that man cannot fly. But it would have been incorrect to have said that it is impossible for man to fly. Today man has proven that this level of thinking is not true. But ask yourself this, in 10 or 20 years from now will you be saying the same thing about something that at present seems impossible to do or accomplish? The intuitive innovative thinker is willing to step out of such a box; do you have the courage too? Being different is not necessarily a bad thing, it is just different! Stagnation has been transformed by those who have been willing to step out of the box, you have this ability just as your colleagues do, but it requires a greater sense of trust from within you. It is not about asking "do I trust another," it is about firstly trusting yourself. From developing self-trust you will find it easier to trust others, as they will you. Mistakes are made, but in those times ask yourself an important question: "what is the best teacher?" It is the experience of our own mistakes of course! When you are intuitive you are being spiritual, when you are spiritual you are being intuitive.

WHAT IS MEDITATION?

Meditation is the expression of the intelligence that links life and form. Meditation is a technique of the mind which helps to produce a correct and clear relationship to align the inner-self. Meditation helps to calm down the entire central nervous system by quietening the mind. Meditation is a way to establish a direct channel between the universe and the Soul's expression through the Spirit. It is a method which helps to purify your lower personality giving you an opportunity to reason with yourself and life without being caught up in logic. People in general are not yet ready or willing to follow this inner pathway. Many choose to continually work and think using their logic and the lower energy fields only. The main purpose of meditation is to develop a greater awareness of how your lower personality works. This will help you to develop clear ways of thinking in order for you to take greater control over the Ego and emotions. One of the positive effects of meditation is that it brings greater stability and health to you on all levels.

The science of the breath is of key importance in relation to meditation. See chapters *"The breath"* and *"Breathing techniques."* Your consciousness controls your breath and the breath controls your life force. Meditation is a tool that you can use to advance your understanding of how to use the breath in all levels of life. You can for example breathe through your fears in order to lessen their impact upon you.

Light is consciousness. When you call for the light, then you call for your life force. The practice of meditation has a direct connection to your consciousness. Your consciousness controls the central nervous system and the heartbeat. Meditation can help relax the heart. This then decreases the blood pressure and you automatically become more energy efficient. The power of meditation is limitless because it connects you more directly to the universal flow of life. You can only access its power by actively asking for it. In order for you to understand the depth of meditation you must first learn to be still and present. See chapter "*How to meditate.*"

THE FREEDOM THAT MEDITATION BRINGS TO YOUR MIND, BODY AND SOUL

If you are afraid of stepping into the unknown or are escaping the higher Self, then it is wise to first overcome this fear before you can discover the freedom that is achieved through meditation. Fear of your higher Self is the jail master of the soul. When you develop your meditation skills, then you will move closer to transforming the controlling aspect of your logical mind and your Ego. The Divine within you is like a fresh water spring that is waiting to be released from the lower mind, the Ego and emotions. Logic and emotions can dominate your life force but if you meditate then it is a clear indication that you are ready for liberation and transformation.

One of the main reasons why we are on Earth is to develop spiritual values and to live by them with every breath. Meditation is a discipline that takes you closer to that purpose as it brings changes on many levels within and around the physical body. Meditation works directly and indirectly to balance the entire central nervous system. This harmonises you positively. Meditation allows you to feel the freedom of independence. It is after all, your journey. No other person can be where you are or do what you are doing during these moments of meditation. It is your decisions, your actions and your thoughts that create your journey in life. Meditation is one of many tools that can be used to raise consciousness, simply by re-directing your thoughts. All it takes is your permission.

All memories are held within the unconscious, but do you pay attention to how the memory works and impacts your life? A basic example of this is if you were asked "what is your telephone number?" Your reply would be brought out from your memory – the unconscious – into the conscious in order to answer. Your consciousness has, in this example, entered the memory bank of the unconscious to draw out that data. You could say that it is like going to your memory bank and withdrawing a certain amount of memory from your memory account. You know it is there, but it is sleeping until it is required. Here are some questions you can ask yourself regarding your memory bank in order to understand more deeply how you access it:

- How easy is it to access what you require?

- Has something or someone got into your memory account to alter things? Some people can be very persuasive and the result can be that you change your opinion. If so, how do you then use this memory? Do you use it as it was or as it now seems to be?

- What value do you put on your memory account? Do you store wisdom or do you store gossip and judgement?

- Do your memories keep you in the past?

- Do your memories create fear of the future?

- Where is my consciousness when I am being present? Do you for example recall a past memory or experience in order to evaluate the present situation? Does the previous experience have relevance for the present situation or is it only a playback of old memories stopping you from going forward?

ACCESSIBILITY

Your memory has a big impact on how you behave and under what conditions you have been living your life. How you use your memories depends to a great degree on what you have been taught or told to do. Fear will continue to influence your behaviour patterns until you begin to take greater responsibility for your choices and actions. To transform yourself, you have to take control over your negative memories. This means learning to be present without the interference of negative past memories. If you place your negative memories in a safety deposit box where they cannot interfere with your current account, then you may be escaping those feelings. But they are still there, and at some time that deposit box may be opened when you cannot protect yourself from them. They may for example appear if you have a traumatic experience or if you are going through difficult times.

WHAT IS THE UNCONSCIOUS WHERE MEMORIES ARE STORED?

There is much written about the conscious qualities of the mind. But what is the unconscious and in what way does it affect us in our daily living? If you look up the word unconscious, then you might find the following: "*temporarily lacking consciousness, lacking awareness and the capacity for sensory perception, or without conscious control; involuntary or unintended.*" You most likely know, even if not from experience, how a person looks when they are unconscious. The brain's sensory perception has been cut off for a period of time. This can occur for example when a boxer is knocked out. The state of being unconscious is also witnessed more profoundly when a person is in a coma. Both examples are recognised as being unconscious.

If someone has persuaded you to do something that you are concerned about then that will interfere with what you feel is correct for you. It may impact your conscious, because your deeper thoughts (the unconscious) hold information about what is true to you. Your conscious may struggle for a while to sort it out, which is where the unconscious feeling or thought can be very strong. It is highly likely that this will create a great deal of stress for you because you are being untrue to the Self by not letting the unconscious guide you along the right path.

YOUR PRINCIPLES OF LIFE

The values you hold determine the life you live and what you have created around those inner values. Memories can play a vital role in your life. Positive and negative memories will impact your memory account and because of that they will have an effect of everyday living. These values will determine in which areas you spend your life energy.

All past memories are points of your own history, some are stronger than others. Because memories are held in the unconscious, the unconscious requires permission from the conscious part of your brain to open that account in order to access their values and content. What is then the value or use associated with this? There can be great joy in past memories, which is true for the opposite, where there may lay a lot of negative energy. If your conscious does not give you permission to enter these past memories, then they may be there for a very long time. This can happen if you have experienced a trauma and have stored those memories away. You can access the keys that will help release any trauma that is present by entering meditation with a clear intention to open the door to that past happening. If it is not accessible this way, then there might be therapies that can help release it.

PAST MEMORIES BLOCKING FUTURE EVENTS

A negative past memory that is locked away in the unconscious may prevent you from making a decision due to the fear or unpleasant feeling that is connected to it. An example of that could be that you do not want to go alone for a swim because you fear drowning. This fear can be connected to something that has happened earlier in your life, but it could also be connected to a past life experience.

THE UNINTENDED THOUGHTS

It might be difficult to comprehend the unintended thoughts and the involuntary movement of your body. Let us look at how this impacts life. The involuntary or unintended behaviour could be interpreted as not being aware of your actions and behaviour. This is the unconscious at work. The involuntary act is an unconscious happening that can be triggered by a natural instinct. Much of nature follows the natural instinct. An example: a Cheetah is hunting a Gazelle. The Cheetah gets very close to the Gazelle, and in a moment they both freeze. The Gazelle instinctively feels fear and decides to run. Until that moment the Cheetah remained motionless, but in that second when the Gazelle's instinct came in and started to run, it kick started the unconscious instinct of the Cheetah to chase in order to catch its prey. To a degree the human being also has such a natural instinct that rises from the unconscious, but a person's higher consciousness can override the natural instinct of fear.

Have you experienced answering without thinking? Whenever you do that you are actually being true to your Self, but those around you may not like what you have expressed. Other people's buttons are often pushed in this way. The unconscious holds an infinite amount of information and wisdom that is part of your memory account. Much of this comes from experiences, because your experiences are your best teachers. How can you open this up whilst still being present? To be still and reflect on it (contemplate) is a very good way to get access to the knowledge that is held in the unconscious. When you are contemplating, then your mind is using both the left and the right sides of the brain. It is actively using the logical thinking and at the same time being relaxed enough to have access to the right side, as in a meditation. When you are meditating, your consciousness is being directed into your higher consciousness – the fourth dimension, your spiritual qualities. When you are being logical, your consciousness is directed into the third dimension, your physical qualities. Contemplation lies between the meditative state and the logic, from where the view of both the higher and lower consciousnesses will complement each other. You may have experienced this when taking a walk alone in nature while your mind seems to be somewhere else. You can on such occasions work through things and try to find solutions, without stress. This is contemplation.

Meditation is another good way to access greater knowledge. When in a meditative state the logic cannot interfere with the meditative process. What you access will not be influenced or corrupted by the logic, nor will it be corrupted by your emotions. It is also a good place to be in to help resolve problems. Your lower consciousness usually continues to go round and round with the problem endlessly. Meditation will allow your consciousness to see into situations without interference from the lower consciousness and to come to a solution, free from interference from your logic.

Rewiring your mind

This chapter will help you understand how the consciousness of your logical mind can be rewired by taking control of, and directing your thoughts. Two aspects are important to understand about a person's relationship with their thoughts:

1. There are people who are comfortable witnessing their thoughts.

2. There are people who think they are their thoughts.

By learning to observe your thoughts, you will become more aware of your neural circuitry. This is the system that passes messages between different parts of the brain to make you choose what to do with those messages. By observing your reactions, you learn to change to another response. One danger of getting involved with your thoughts can be that your emotional energy may rise into your thoughts and cause confusion. Learning to observe your thoughts is a skill needed in order for you to enter higher consciousness activity, and from here you can direct your thoughts without the control of the lower consciousness.

Reference

Can you consciously rewire your brain with your thoughts? Yes you can and you do. You can change your thought patterns through your conscious efforts to rewire how the neuron-circuits connect. This is essentially down to choice. You have the right to decide not to connect to a circuitry (way of thinking) that causes stress. You can choose to feed the one that is serving the right side of the brain instead. For example, when the anger circuit wants to run again, you may not like the way it feels inside the body, so you may say "NO" to its running. Every time the anger circuit gets triggered and wants to run again, you can bring your attention back to it. You do not like the way anger feels, so you can shut it down by continuing to say "NO" to it time after time until it no longer appears. For example, if you were to say to yourself "I will never again get angry at another driver," you can watch for when that moment appears, and what you choose to do in that moment will confirm (one way or the other) whether your rewiring has worked – anger or no anger. When you continually practice this method, that particular circuit of the brain will rarely run again, because you are stopping it as soon as it starts. You will learn that this can be successfully applied to other issues you may have, such as jealousy. You will also learn that certain thoughts stimulate the emotional energies, which can result in a mental response, and anger is one such response. If you study the physiological responses you make in relation to your thoughts and emotions, and the end result of your thoughts, then you can learn and change much in your life pattern.

It might help you to look at your brain as a kind of computer network. It may then be easier to understand how to rewire your mind. You change the programming. But you have to be willing and strong to make change happen. All humans have the ability to focus their minds on what they want to think about. You decide that, no one else.

IT IS IMPORTANT TO SLEEP

The brain needs sleep. When your brain and body cells have been traumatised, you can feel totally burned out and want to sleep. Sleep is good for your mind and your body. If you listen to what your mind and body are telling you, then much can be healed, it is that simple. When you are under stress, this is usually time-achievement orientated. The left hemisphere can then become traumatised as it is continually seeking ways to solve problems or issues. This often causes the left brain's responses to become less functional due to the stress factor. It is when you rest and learn to breathe through stressful times and traumatic circumstances that you will help take out dominating negative thoughts that are preventing the right hemisphere from functioning properly. This basically means that you can, through the proper use of the breath, calm down your thoughts. You can learn to let go of them and to seek a new course of thought. In this manner you make the right side of the brain dominate your left. The higher consciousness is stress free because it does not follow physical laws. When you use your higher consciousness then there are no expectations of your Self.

DOES MEDITATION HELP?

Those who meditate are willing to pay attention to their thoughts so that they can purposefully redirect their mind (logic) into the higher consciousness activity. This teaches the mind to think in another way. For example, consciously thinking about how you breathe is a tool that provides the brain with an alternative to the constant brain chatter. It permits the mind to focus on breathing rather than something else. Learning to observe your thoughts and not engage with them is a skill you can learn by becoming the observer of yourself.

WHAT IS THE DIFFERENCE BETWEEN BEING SOLID AND FLUID?

We view the world as being either solid or fluid. You get up in the morning and take a walk in the woods. Then you may stop and notice the sunlight that comes through the trees, the grass and the sparkling drops of water on the grass. Everything is vivid, beautiful and connected. You feel that you are a part of it; you are in its flow. All is one and one is all! That is very different from saying "I am solid, and that is a tree, the blades of grass and the drops of water on the grass are all separate." Solid is being logical. Logic separates things and puts them into boxes. Being fluid is being at one with all things. The sky, the trees, grass and water are seen as a combined energy. How do you see the world?

HOW TO CHANGE FROM SOLID TO FLUID?

Being stiff or without flexibility causes you to become too solid in life. You then find it difficult to accept and blend with other people and nature. Logic makes you think in solid ways because it is a square way of thinking. It judges and separates. The intuitive, higher mind has a flow. This is a fluidity that brings joy to all thoughts of life. In this aspect of consciousness you feel that you are a part of everything. You are connected. There is oneness. The mind can be rewired to accept both concepts to remain strong and solid in your logic as well as being fluid and focused on your higher consciousness. This leads to mastering the art of being present.

Meditation definitely helps in this process, but the circuits in your brain require the right input of thought in order to achieve any change in this area. Changing old ways of thinking is not an easy thing to do, but it can be done. You learn to break old habits by first saying "NO" to them. You also say *"I am the observer of my thoughts and therefore I am the creator of my life."* I decide, (not choose) what occurs next! I can open a new line of thought that will create peace in my life.

All individuals have eight senses, five physical (smell, touch, taste, sight and hearing), and three higher senses (clairvoyance, clairaudience and clairsentience). The responses of your physical senses determine how you experience life in your physical body. The higher senses are experienced through your higher consciousness, which enables your spiritual values to be experienced through your physical Self. The physical senses and the higher senses are complementary. Let us first look individually at the physical senses from an energy point of view.

SMELL: the sense of smell automatically puts you in touch with the environment you are in. You also use your smell when eating and drinking. Your sense of smell can direct you towards or away from something that may smell good or bad.

TOUCH: distance is broken by touch. One of the most intimate things you can do is to touch another person. You step directly into that person's world by touching them.

TASTE: can you imagine what life would be like without being able to taste anything? No bitter, sour, salty and sweet sensations on the tongue. It is interesting to note that the sweet senses are at the very front of the tongue. Taste is closely connected to sight, as is often said that "you eat with your eyes."

Reference

SIGHT: the sense of sight is of great importance in all aspects of your life. There are two levels of how you view the world - the physical, and the spiritual. Your logic uses the physical eyes to view the world from a physical perspective and it connects to the left hemisphere of the brain. It is not the eyes that determine what you see; it is the brain that determines what you choose to see. The beauty of what you see, such as a sunset, gives you an experience that feeds the soul.

HEARING: hearing is the first of the five senses to be activated. For example, a baby hears the heartbeat of its mother whilst being carried in her womb. The baby feels and hears every vibration that comes within its area. Hearing helps provide direction as to where a certain sound comes from.

Your higher senses are clairvoyance, clairaudience and clairsentience. These senses are activated when your higher consciousness is opened. It is as if a light has been put on in a room and you can see more clearly what is there. This will then lead you to start to look for answers outside the box thinking (logic). This will in turn help stimulate your higher senses and intuition. For example, you may experience an uplifting moment without being aware of why you feel as you do. You are simply happier.

HERE IS A BRIEF DESCRIPTION OF THE THREE HIGHER SENSES.

CLAIRVOYANCE: your inner vision focuses inwardly for in-sights rather than looking outside for solutions. You are in this way creating a stronger link to the right side of your brain. Clairvoyance is connected to your spiritual eye which is known as "Third Eye." The third eye is a metaphysical energy that is one of seven energy centres (chakras) that are present in the physical body. The third eye is to be found in the middle of your forehead. Your spiritual eye is connected to the right side of the brain and higher consciousness. When this centre is activated it can sometimes feel as if there is a mild pressure being put on the middle of your forehead. Seeing the world through your spiritual eye gives you a holistic view of life. Your spiritual eye is connected to your physical eyes and the visual cortex at the back of your head.

CLAIRAUDIENCE: when the sensitivity of the energy centre located in the lower part of your throat is activated, you may find that your intuition becomes stronger. You may experience this as a sensation of inner hearing, and it may take some time and practice to adjust to its vibration.

CLAIRSENTIENCE: this sense is deeply connected to your ability to sense the spiritual force of yourself and others around you. The quality of clairsentience is very much about listening more deeply to your feelings and intuition. You know when something is right, you can feel it!

HOW DO INTUITION AND LOGIC INTERACT WITH ALL SENSES?

You will until the moment of spiritual awakening mainly use your logic and the five physical senses. Your consciousness is at the third dimension (3D). You may at this level be happy and balanced in your life, but you may also have a lot of fear. In moments of awakening you may experience strong feelings and some of these questions may become relevant:

- Is there more to life than what I am experiencing at this moment?

- Do I have a spirit and soul?

- Is there such a thing as eternal life?

- How can I learn to trust my gut feeling?

- How can I quieten my mind?

- What is meditation?

- Why am I here?

When these questions arise and you direct your consciousness and focus on these questions, then the brain receives more light energy from universal consciousness. The light then stimulates the pineal and pituitary glands in the head, causing them to awaken your higher consciousness of the fourth dimension. This is the beginning of your spiritual development, where your higher consciousness will seek ways in which to communicate clearly with your logical self. This is where the battle between logic and intuition begins.

One of the main differences between intuition and logic is that your intuition is not controlled by physical laws. The intuition, your higher consciousness, understands perfectly how logic functions through the five senses and physical laws, but logic does not and cannot comprehend how intuition works in accordance to your higher consciousness and senses. When you only use your logic you do not have access to the tools of Self realisation. The Ego is sceptical and is logically reasoning from the left side of your brain. When you only use your logic, then you have difficulty in understanding or trusting what you cannot feel or see with your physical senses. This is mainly due to the fact that the logical thought is based upon the premise of past, present and future. A negative past experience may for example create a fear of the experience being repeated sometime in the future. This may lead to you trying to make the future safe in order to protect yourself from a possible repeat of a negative previous experience. You can then become lost in the past and future and you are not able to experience the present moment.

When you become intuitive, however, you will have developed a greater sense of trust and have little or no fear. When you trust the Self, then controlling factors created by your logic will be minimised. This will take you more deeply into trusting your feelings and you will not hesitate to step into the unknown. Your feelings are taking you to the light. That gut feeling touches your higher consciousness, giving you an opportunity to listen more deeply and to follow your thoughts from within. It can be like having an innovative flash, an inspired idea that may even seem far out or beyond the concept you are working on. If that intuitive thought is not directly acted upon it will have passed. The moment is lost and it becomes history. However if you hold that innovative idea within the right hemisphere of your brain, it may well flourish through you seeking to be more creative with it. You may also experience that your logic doubts what your intuitive insight has just provided you with. If you are being logical about an intuitive thought then you may lose it, simply because the idea goes beyond logical comprehension.

Greater harmony and peace will be present within your whole being when the intuitive and logical qualities of your consciousness have blended. Fear will no longer be present to control your thoughts. Your emotions will be balanced, allowing you to intuit clear feelings and not clouded ones. Positive thought creates positive action. Your intuitive quality gives you opportunities to follow such a path; to experience the unknown as it unfolds before you can confirm that your positive thought and action were right. To begin and maintain such a flow in your life may at first not seem to be easy. But small steps and small beginnings are a part of the learning. To accept and be patient with whatever you are working with at any given moment in your life are qualities that can be developed from within your Self. All of your senses will be used in a complementary way when you listen to your intuitive self. This is because your higher consciousness does not block out the logic. Logic on the other hand tries to block your higher consciousness as it cannot understand it. When logic and intuition blend and work together they give you a clear, balanced life. Then you will have truly stepped out of the box thinking (logic) and followed your inner Self. You have faith in your Self and you hold peace, joy and love.

THE ATTRACTION OF PAIN

WHAT IS PAIN?

Pain is a natural happening that warns the physical body that something is wrong somewhere. There are three main forms of pain. They are *physical, emotional and mental*. All three play specific roles in the unfolding of human experiences because all three have a profound effect upon the physical body. Let us go deeper into the meaning of these three forms of pain.

PHYSICAL PAIN

"Direct physical pain" is the most obvious to be noticed. An example is when you damage the skin by cutting yourself, burning or falling on your knee. We call these injuries, and each injury gives us a degree of pain. How much pain you feel is dependent on two main factors.

1. How deep the wound is.

2. How extensive the injury is (as in surface area of the skin and underlying tissue).

How we receive or even attract physical pain is very individual, but one thing for sure is that it makes us stop for a while. Again this depends upon how severe the pain is and how quickly it can be healed. Some priests have been known to purge themselves of impurities through self-inflicted pain. This was done by lashing themselves over their shoulders and across their backs with a whip, causing lacerations that would leave scars. Some people take revenge on others by inflicting pain upon them.

EMOTIONAL PAIN

This kind of pain is not as obvious as physical pain because it is not directly a physical phenomenon. By its nature, emotional pain could be described as a secondary pain. For example when you become emotionally upset about something your emotions create vibrations which can be felt as pain. If the nerve endings are vibrating strongly they will pass on the message to tell the physical body that you are in pain. Let us look at an example. If you are deeply emotionally attached to someone and if that person leaves you, you may well go through the pain of emotional detachment. Your attachments of needing that person in your life are so strong that you cannot bear the thought of being without them. This affects your solar plexus and the organs within that area. You may for example develop an eating disorder. You may also develop headaches or slight depression. The emotions are good at creating secondary pain as a means of telling you that your needs and wishes are so strong that they can become painful if not fulfilled. When you become emotionally upset, you attract pain. This is an inbuilt system that helps to notify you that something is lacking, or that your needs are far greater than your acceptance of your situation. Pain can arise whenever your emotions are in disharmony. They do so to help you understand that something is wrong. If you invite fear to enter, your fear will direct the body to become painful. Fear will create illusions that are painful. Even the illusions of pleasure will be the same as pain for you.

MENTAL PAIN

Do you think it is right that your mistakes are reasonable grounds for depression, disillusionment are relative attack on what you think has failed you? The attraction of pain to the mental body is often brought about by guilt. The guilt makes the body the servant of pain. This is a part of the Ego's heavy investment in the physical body. The Ego justifies itself by saying "you are suffering and are in pain because of what you did or are doing." Mental pain can also be caused by stress factors which another person may be creating for you.

HOW THE ATTRACTION OF PAIN WORKS

What you send to others you send to yourself. So if you cause others pain, then you cause pain to yourself. All of your feelings are given to you by the sender (you), and are received by you. This is the mirror effect. The Ego and the Spirit both recognise this. When your Spirit tells you this is joy, the Ego hides it. Your Ego wants to keep you unaware of joy because it seeks to control you. For example, if you are expecting someone you like to be at a gathering of friends, and that person does not show up, you may feel sad, lost or even depressed. Then the Ego will stop you from being present with the friends you are spending time with. Your thoughts and feelings will be drifting away, probably to something in the past or in the future. You become lost and cut off from the moment. The Ego's messages are always sent away from you, in the belief that the message of attack or injury will cause suffering and pain to others rather than to the Self. And even if you suffer, someone else will suffer more. An example here is that if you block or deny giving someone credit for a job well done, you are preventing yourself from sharing your natural joy and happiness for that person. This could be because you may be jealous of that person.

The Ego and the Holy Spirit are both senders and receivers. For what is sent through you will return to you. In this way the Ego finds the reward it seeks, returning it to you time after time in the form of pain until the light is seen. There is no separation. You are at one with everything. However, in the logical world there are dualities that can and do coexist in peace. Search for their truth through higher-mind principles and not lower mind consciousness. Only then will the release of the emotional nature and lower-mind principles appear to be transformed in their many forms. The transformation of the Ego on your path in life is of key importance to transforming any form of pain you may be holding, by bringing peace to the Self!

THE BREATH

The breath is an automatic happening that could be de-scribed as a miracle of life. Your body would not be able to function without the voluntary use of the physical breath. But why are we breathing? The different steps of breathing are explained in "The four stages of breathing." How your breath can transform and heal is explained in the section *"The therapeutic understanding and use of the breath."*

THE FOUR STAGES OF BREATHING

THE IN-BREATH: is a spontaneous happening, as the soul wishes to maintain the life force of the physical body through the spirit. It is an unconscious effort to draw new life via the oxygen into the lungs. The lungs will fill in accordance to your physical needs as you take your in-breath. The need will vary, for example if you are running or meditating. There is new opportunity with each in-breath, depending on how you choose to use the energy that is derived from it. It is the breath of life!

THE PAUSE BETWEEN THE IN-BREATH AND THE OUT-BREATH: a mo-mentary pause comes when the in-breath is complete. The length of this pause is determined by where you are with yourself. For example, if you are calm or if you are angry. Most of the time you are breathing unconsciously, but you can also learn to use the pause between the breaths in a way

Reference

that may serve you better. An example of this is when you choose not to respond immediately to a person who may be angry with you. You hold your breath for a moment longer before replying. This will give you enough time to reflect on your response. It is also interesting to note that the pause between each breath is where most decisions are made. It is here that the energy of the in-breath directs the consciousness that creates the physical reactions you experience.

THE OUT-BREATH: this aspect of breathing is connected to the release of old energy that has been used. This is the "breath of death" as it releases the old. The old does not only contain carbon dioxide and water, but it can be used in a therapeutic way too. This is explained later on.

THE PAUSE BETWEEN THE OUT-BREATH AND THE NEW IN-BREATH: it is here that there is a secondary moment, i.e. a pause that prepares you for what to do next.

THE THERAPEUTIC UNDERSTANDING AND USE OF THE BREATH:

Each in-breath holds the opportunity to be positive, crea-tive, intuitive or innovative. It can also be used in a destruc-tive and negative way. So what determines this? The short answer is consciousness. Your thoughts are the electrically charged energy that determines how you use your life force that comes within each breath. Here is a very simplistic view of how it works. You take an in-breath that feeds the lungs with oxygen and then enters the blood stream to help give life to the heart. The heart then pumps the oxygen-rich blood around the physical body to create life as we know it. There are many hidden factors to be explained here. The first thing to realise is that breath is consciousness. This can be explained by the fact that the breath enables you to speak your intentions though the spoken word in order to help you communicate with others. Communication through the spoken word comes via the out-breath. This is because the out-breath is clearing old energies and thoughts as you speak to others. Your words become history as soon as you have expressed them.

It is wise to take some time before responding in order to process what you wish to say, or how to respond. Between the in-breath and the out-breath is where the "pause" comes into play. In this limited time space, the mind and often the emotions are looking for ways to respond to events. How long you are able to hold or maintain that pause largely determines how and in which way you will use the energy of the in-breath to respond to the situation. Let us say that you are in a rush. Then your reactions and energy (breathing) will be focused on achieving what is required in the quickest possible way. So your breathing is likely to be short and quick, as are your actions. But on the other hand if you were to allow yourself to be more relaxed, you would be calmer and possibly more collected in your thoughts and actions. Your breathing would also be more relaxed and you would give yourself more time to think. Then your reactions will come from a greater sense of peace. Just as important is that you would not react so quickly to a situation because you have decided to be efficient with your breath and hold it for a little bit longer before responding. This slightly longer pause can be very empowering as you will not rush into anything if someone "pushes your buttons." In those extra moments the whole world could change and so could your thoughts about it, because you will have managed your breathing technique to suit the situation. Another example is that if you were emotionally imbalanced then your emotional body has a definite affect upon your breathing by quickening it during the moments of rising emotion. This is a natural happening. But how do you master the breath to help balance both examples given here? See chapter *"Breathing techniques."*

THE EGO - POISON OF THE SOUL

The Ego is a creation of your mind and emotions. The Ego creates illusions through the use of fear in order to control a person's life. There are two forms of Ego that come from the same source. There is the Ego of the lower personality, and the Spiritual Ego. The Ego in both aspects seeks recognition to hold on to its identity. The Ego feeds off the recognition it receives. The Ego is forever power-hungry for more and more of the same and seeks to control you by blocking your intuition. It does this by stopping you from being present. In this way, the access to your higher Self is weakened. When you have a spiritual Ego then it is an indication that you have not completely transformed your lower nature and that there is still some inner work to be done. The Ego is a negative source of energy because it seeks to prevent you from serving others by keeping you in the dark. The Ego controls what it wishes to see and hear. It does this by continually seeking to hold you in the energies of fear and judgement. Past experiences and future projections are then manipulated through your emotions and fear in order to confuse logic and make the mind believe in the illusions that fear creates. Fear and judgment prevent you from being present. The present is the only place the Ego cannot be, because it would be out of control.

JEALOUSY – is one of the most destructive forces that you can hold.

JUDGEMENT – is a logical perception of the world. Through the consciousness of judgement you see the world as black or white, right or wrong. It is a very destructive energy that has outlived its purpose because it now creates separation. The dualities of black or white at first gave the basic structure on which to choose. However this thought pattern is no longer relevant to current social structures. The evidence of its destructive ways is that people continue to harm each other through judgement, such as saying "I don't like you, or "your religion is no good." Whenever people are separated from being true to each other, then the true spirit of life is not of the light, it is of darkness. No one person can judge another.

FEAR – is Ego-based. It is a negative force that seeks to take you away from trusting the Self by creating doubt in your heart and mind. You may find that the source of your fear is deeply hidden in your emotions.

ENVY – is shown when you want what someone else has but may not be willing to work for it, for example. Envy is deeply connected to your needs. Needy people are most envious because they are continually seeking answers from outside themselves and as such see little value in what they already have. Envy and jealously are closely linked.

GREED – is a deep emotional and spiritual dissatisfaction. You can never have enough. Such a hole will never be filled as long as the individual continues to seek rewards.

COMPARISON – the Ego always seeks to compare. It is the mirror of you towards others. You may feel superior (look at me) or inferior (hide yourself) and as such may wish to be like another person or not.

INSECURITY – is a deep lack of trust, a mental instability, emotional instability or lack of light, spirit and soul awareness.

The Ego's purpose is to create a separation from your Soul – your light force – and the harmony it brings to your mind and heart. The Ego cannot stay in the present; it would be out of a job. It can only stay in control when you are either in the past or future time zones. This is due to the fact that the past and future are open to past experiences and the assumptions and speculations of futuristic happenings. It is here that the Ego plays on your fears. For example fear comes from past experiences that can be hidden in the subconscious. The Ego can use that past experience to prevent you from entering a new experience by convincing you that it may be too dangerous to venture into that area. It will use that negative experience of the past to convince you that it will happen again, thus keeping you under its control. In this manner the Ego also seeks to control the possible future, although it has a fascination for it. It will always seek to know what the future represents by trying to control it, which of course is not a reality. What it does not know, it will try to make it safe. This is why you often over protect yourself in a number of ways. For example, fear may overpower you from climbing a tree or learning to ice skate because fear tells you that you will fall. Or you may over protect another person by continually interfering with their choices. Your intentions may be good, but you may be preventing that person from an experience that they need to have in order to develop and grow. For more information on how to transform the Ego – see chapter "*Ego.*"

THE EMOTIONAL BODY

The term "emotional body" is slightly misleading. It gives the idea of something with a specific shape or form. The emotions you feel come from different areas of you. Examples of emotions are anger, fear or sexual needs and desires. However they all join to become a collective energy that is referred to as "the emotional body." This is a metaphysical energy field located outside of your physical body in the area of the solar plexus. The emotional body is a mixture of forces that are working through the consciousness of a person in the form of for example fear, desire, expectations, judgement, determinations, incentives and projections. The understanding of these forces is much of what modern psychology is based on. There are also positive emotions that can be felt, such as when you feel happy to be with someone or during a funeral when relaxing your feeling of love for someone who has passed away. The emotional body is the prime motivating factor in the lives of the majority of people today. It collectively feels every sound and vibration, due to the facts that the emotional body is where most people are centring their consciousness at present. It is the most developed body of energy in most people at this point of evolution. The emotional body receives a large amount of the life energy because the emotions are strongly felt in many life situations. To a large extent the physical experiences that are felt through or by the emotional body are based on emotional

Reference

needs, such as wanting another person to love you. This is expressed through the physical (logical) experience that the person has from their emotions. The logic is primarily fixed on desires of the physical self, and will protect its interests at all costs. The person who seeks to change emotional behaviour patterns must seek higher consciousness principles. It is important to note that the lower nature (logic, Ego and emotions) does not have the tools to transform itself. It is impossible to transform or heal emotions with emotions or fear with fear. The emotional body is the prime energy to be transformed in all people. It is the most alive and powerful. Many people use this energy in combination with their sexual feelings and become confused due to the strong energy of emotions which becomes an emotional sexuality rather than the pure sexuality.

The emotional body has a great impact on the central nervous system. This is often felt in the stomach area. Emotional turmoil for example can produce great solar plexus difficulties due to the energies that meet in the emotional body. It is from this area that various conflicts arise within a person who is trying to balance their emotions. This centre is also affected by the Moon and its cycles. The full Moon can have a strong influence upon the solar plexus, especially in those whose lives are based in the solar plexus. The emotions can also have a strong influence upon the sexual nature, causing over simulation of that area. The emotional body is both a great reflector and receiver of energies. It takes in all colours, sounds and movement from the surroundings. The emotional body receives the imprints of every desire; it contacts every need in the nearby environment. Thought sets the emotional body in motion and every sound causes it to vibrate.

The emotional body is also closely aligned with the physical willpower and logic. Over use of the physical willpower drains the body of energy. It can also have a strong negative effect on the central nervous system. If an individual continues to use physical willpower for a long period of time to manifest what they want in life, the effects can be very damaging. Mental problems, depression, strong nervous tension, addictions of all kinds, stomach troubles and cancers can arise from the overstimulation of willpower and emotional imbalance. Through the practice of higher consciousness awakening, the emotional body will gradually transform and become clear. The Ego can no longer corrupt your feelings and will be powerless. This can be achieved by learning to hold back emotional forces. One way to do this is to receive and register only those impressions which come from the intuition. By developing your awareness in this way, the controlling powers of the emotional body will gradually disappear as less emotional energy is present. Then you are free to understand your emotions from your truth. The higher consciousness will then mirror correctly what you need to feel and see. You will then move forward through a positive force. You are no longer just blowing in the winds of thought, or rising with the tide of desire and needs. Real change can happen when correct discipline of higher consciousness is applied to the emotional body.

WHAT WORDS CAN DESCRIBE THE EMOTIONAL BODY?

When it is clear from negative energies, the emotional body is best described as still, serene, unruffled, quiet, at rest or of a mirror-like quality - the surface of which is like a clear watery reflector. It is a centre that accurately transmits the wishes and aims of the higher self and not the controlling needs and desires of the lower personality.

It is clear to see from the above that in order to master the emotional body, you must fully understand its forces. The purpose is to understand and balance the emotional body so that it no longer controls you. Everything that is stated in the *"Fear and control"* section is relevant for study. You will then begin to understand what negative forces you hold in your emotional body. The aim is to have the emotional body mastered from your higher Self. As your feelings pass through you, you study and understand them in seconds by taking them to your higher mind instead of keeping them in the lower floors of the emotions and logical thinking. From there you can see clearly what is occurring. You have put your inner light into these feelings and are seeking answers through the clarity of higher consciousness and intuition. Here are some things for you to consider when clearing your emotional body of negative energies:

- Constantly watch the desires, motives and the wishes that cross your horizon. This will help lead you to work with a higher order of thought and not be lost in the logic.

- Try to be in contact with your higher Self (truth, love, acceptance, forgiveness) and to reflect this in your daily living. At first mistakes will be made, until little by little a positive building process of choices and decisions will take shape. Such actions will allow you to reach up into the higher guidance that all people seek. It is from this level of higher consciousness that you will find the release of the Ego's emotional control factors.

- Take a daily practice of stilling the emotional body. Do this by focusing on it with thoughts of stillness whilst breathing the breath of calmness. Much is said of stilling the mind, but we should remember that by stilling the emotional body you are taking a step nearer to quietening the mind. One follows the other, and it is indeed wise to begin at the bottom of the ladder of consciousness.

• Create a new life rhythm. Part of the process of inner development is to look at whether you find it easier to be in a positive or negative vibration. Identify situations where you feel fear, worry, desires of any kind, emotional love of anything or anyone, discouragement, and oversensitivity to other people's opinion of you. When you look deeply at all these issues then you may look for ways to overcome those negative vibrations by imposing a new positive rhythm on them. A positive rhythm will eliminate those negative forces whilst at the same time create a constructive view of life instead. See chapter "*Rewiring your mind.*"

It is wise to remember that the process of clearing out and harmonising the emotional body is usually gradual. This is because the polarisation of consciousness is shifting from one sub-plane to another, from lower to higher consciousness. This is something that rarely happens overnight. The steps are gradual but can be strong. There will be certain tests that will occur either at night or during the day in this transitional period. These are the first small initiations, and can be as simple as a realisation of how you may be behaving emotionally. This will eventually lead to a second greater change, such as deciding to change your behavioural pattern, leading you to mastering your emotions. When this transformation has been fully accomplished, you will then stand free from any emotional influences. For example other people's projections of their emotional energy cannot have an influence on you and they can therefore not control you through their emotions. You will understand how forces of this nature appear, but you will no longer be influenced by, or lost in them. Then you will no longer be drawn into fears.

The clarity of higher consciousness has mastered the lower nature and you stand free in the Light.

THE MIRROR EFFECT

WHAT IS THE MIRROR EFFECT?

Everyone is a mirror of someone else. This can be understood when you recognise and accept that what you send out will at some point return to you as a message. Because what you do to others you do to yourself. Why would someone judge another person if they knew they were judging themselves? Who would be angry at another person if they knew they were being angry at themselves? What you experience in life if something that you have asked for on some level. You may not directly recognise it as something you have asked for, as you may not fully understand how cause and effect, action and reaction impact you and others. Your logical perception, feelings, emotions and Ego often block you from seeing and reading the message that the mirror is trying to show you. This may be because you do not want to take responsibility for the choices you make. You often make Ego-based choices in denial of your truth. The Ego is a master of disguise and always looks outside itself. This could be to blame another person for what they have said or done to you. It is a form of escape. If you were to stand in front of a full-length mirror and look deeply to yourself, what would you see? Try to look deeper within. There can be thousands of you there, because each experience is a moment of you being somewhere and doing something. This is what memory tells us. It is a kind of a mirror that will bring a picture of a past happening to your mind's eye in order for you to relate to it mentally and often emotionally.

If you were to take a deeper look at the meaning of life you could say that "I am you and you are me." For example, when you have seen a homeless person sleeping on the street, have you ever said to yourself "that could be me; or is it you?" Because on one level that person, "the homeless one," is being a mirror for you. Maybe he or she is there to help you understand how fortunate you may be to have a warm home to go to. It may be easy to fall into the trap of judging that homeless person by perhaps saying "that person should work for a living or get a life like I have." But no one can ever be absolutely sure of anyone's circumstances, or how they got to be where they are. The mirror of that homeless person is there perhaps to help you understand how you may judge another person so easily. Or can you be compassionate and understand by saying to yourself that each and every one of us is on a journey, called life. That homeless person may be there to give you an opportunity to change your own point of view of how you see others. They may seem less fortunate than you, but are they? Everyone is serving in one way or another.

Another way to look at the mirror effect is to see it as a messenger for you. The mirror is a reflection of everything you see, feel and do. But if you were to take it a step above your logical views you may be surprised at what you experience. Everything you experience and receive – consciously or not - you have asked for. When you choose not to take things personally, then the energy and the experience is immediately transformed into something that you can view in a neutral way. This happens because you have decided to accept the energy of the experience in the present moment. You are not lost in a past experience, creating fear of what is presently happening. You do not speculate about the future because of past happenings and fear that they will be repeated. You are then in your power and are free from the influences of the Ego. Then you can ask yourself: "What is this telling me and what can I learn from this experience?" Whenever you approach a situation with this form of consciousness you stay out of the drama and away from being a victim. Then there is an opportunity to learn and grow. You do that through understanding of the situation and by not judging it from the logic or Ego's perspective.

The mirror is always showing you what you require to see, but how you see the reflection and what you do about it can be another thing. Nothing happens by chance. There are times when we may not like what we see or what is being said to us, this is the mirror effect pushing your buttons. If you do not like what is happening you may get defensive and step away from your power of truth. This allows the Ego to take over. Then "The Ego's protection" has kicked in. If for example a colleague was to come up to you and start to argue with you about a work issue, how do you respond, and how have you responded in the past to this person? That person may not be the easiest to get on with. They could be very demanding, and as such will put a lot of pressure on you to finish a certain task. You may have a reason for not finishing what you were meant to finish, but the one who has given you the task in that moment is unaware of this. During your conversation you mention why you were unable to complete your task, but your colleague believes this to be an excuse, and does not accept your true explanation. What was the reason for this and where did your communication break down? The mirror is there, but when it is used to project and blame another or yourself there has to be a deeper meaning for its appearance. For example your reason for not completing a task may be perfectly reasonable, but due to the pressure that your colleague is under, that reason may have become too much for him to take at that moment, hence the explosion of anger or finger-pointing blame. So let us look into the mirror to see yourself through your colleague. He is actually mirroring you in the way he acts. Do you see an angry person who does not accept you being late and thinks that you have bad excuses? Go back and see what you think about yourself in this situation. Do you accept being late? Do you think that you have bad excuses for being late? Maybe your colleague is just mirroring what you think about yourself, but you are hiding? Try to think differently about yourself by accepting yourself and how you have chosen to deliver this specific task. See how this affects the behaviour of others. This is also a clear case of a breakdown in communication that can set all kinds of energies into motion. Expectation comes strongly to mind here, for you and your colleague. The mirror effect gives the opportunity for change to happen in a positive way. By not taking things personally you are naturally moving to "out of the box" thinking. You then create the right space in which to be present by simply thinking in another way about this situation. This will create real change in your work environment or at home.

The Self

WHAT IS THE SELF?

The Self is the true essence of you and a beautiful Divine energy. Self shines through when you are completely true to yourself. Put simply, when you trust the Self you become present. Trust in your Self and you will never have to look for confirmation outside of you. Your Self is love. It should therefore be simple to love yourself and to respect you for the person you are. No? You are not alone. When the Ego is present, you are caught in its perception of who you are. In fact, you may not even like yourself much because you lack self worth.

THE LOGICAL PERCEPTION OF THE SELF

The real meaning of the Self is a conscious understanding of your own being – the true essence of your light. When you are in your logical dimension the Ego is often present and you can be caught in its identity, which is not the same as the Self. In our cultural languages there are variations of self, i.e. myself, yourself, himself or herself. These are descriptions of the Self that help identify you with others. There is nothing wrong with that, just remember that it is based on logic. It is reasonable, in the logical world, to have "an identity" that demonstrates in various ways who you are. It can be related to personal characteristics, body type, interests, individual consciousness and other things that are important in order to characterise a person.

The logic places much emphasis on personalising you so that you know who you are. This is demonstrated, for example, by the fact that you have been labelled with a name, sex, date of birth and place of birth. These are identity tags that have been created by logic and which stay with you throughout your life. These identity tags are important for most social structures today. But if you go back in time, they were not there as part of a person's identity. It was simply not interesting to know which day a person was born on, for example. Whenever you refer to "yourself" you are identifying with the logical concept of you. It is reflective of where the "I" or "me" are in any given situation. Let us discuss the "I" as in Identity. The logic uses the "I" to identify you. You could for example say to another person "This is what I need you to do". This means that you, as one person, can tell another person what they should be doing. This is how you express yourself when you see the world through physical definitions. When you express yourself through your higher senses, then you would more likely say something like "can you please share with me how you see things".

In the logical world you have people that are selfish to varying degrees, from minor to extreme. When you are in your higher consciousness, you are selfless. It is not likely that a person who lives only in the lower dimension is selfless, as their act of selflessness is carried out because they need recognition of some kind. Let us look at the difference between the two concepts and remember that true selflessness can only come from your heart and higher consciousness.

- Have an Ego which is very present, because their needs are fear-based. This is a dominating factor in their lives. It makes them particularly self-centred and egoistic. It is here that you may find the "me, me, me" factor to be strong.

- Are deeply insecure and can often have emotional outbursts when they do not get things their own way.

- Are lacking in trust and will often find it difficult to lend anything that they feel is of value to them without strong reassurances that it will be returned as soon as possible.

- Can be secretive and will often withhold information if they feel that they may lose control of it. This is because they may want the credit. This is one way in which the Ego shows itself.

- Are only concerned about themselves.

- Put their needs before others' needs.

- Have behaviour or attitudes which are motivated by self-interest.

- Do not care for the rights of others, often have little empathy, and can at times be highly inconsiderate in their behaviour.

- Can be unwilling to spend, they are ungenerous.

The selfish person has much to deal with in order to live up to their identity. This can be very tiring for the physical body. The selfish person can be holding deep anger that has not been healed. When you challenge that person to give more, or to be more considerate, the underlying anger may then surface and a loss of control will become obvious. Denial of the Self is a big issue to be resolved by the selfish person. This is because they are not true to their Self and they are denying it. By doing so they are denying the true life force that they have within. It will be impossible to find joy in life because the Self is not shining through. It is also very tiring to live up to the logical concept of the identity, and they may become totally lost in this. The result is a lack of self confidence (outer) and a lack of self worth (inner) which can be clearly seen in a person's behaviour and in the choices a person makes. The latter is extremely serious and can have far-reaching consequences. The person that lacks self worth is deeply insecure and may build all forms of protection around them to disguise their inner insecurity.

People that are selfless:

A person that is selfless is first and foremost always true to their Self. This is the starting point. If you are not true to your Self then you cannot truly be selfless as there will be some element of need involved in your attempt to be selfless. Maybe you need the recognition of others and you therefore give up your share of something? This is not selflessness. You have to be true to your heart! A person that is truly selfless is:

- *Unselfish* – sees the need of others and shares whenever possible.

- *Considerate* – shows concern for the rights, feelings and wellbeing of others.

- *Generous* – willing to share unconditionally.

- *Ego-less* – no ulterior motive to their sharing or actions.

- *Unconditional* – they give without asking for anything in return. It is a selfless form of serving.

It is clear from the above that the selfless person is not motivated by self-interest, greed or fear. It could be said that they are also not materialistic as they are not attached to material things. They may still own things, but because they are not attached to them they may give them up or walk away from them without attachment. So how does one become selfless? Does it mean that you do not care for yourself and always put others before you regardless? No it does not. If you are always true to your Self, then you can be true to others. Being selfless contains a healthy amount of compassion. Compassion is an unconditional state of being. It is the energy of your heart and wherever the heart is, so is love. The selfless person does not sacrifice one thing for another. That is the Ego's interpretation of giving. When you give selflessly you require nothing in return. You give from your heart, and this is true service. When you listen to your heart then you are listening to your Self. The Self requires no interpretation because it is your Soul that is acting to demonstrate the qualities of selflessness. The "I" the "me" the selfish and the selfless are all examples of how you interact with others on a physical plane. When you unfold and develop your Self towards higher consciousness, then your identity and the control of your Ego is dropped.

HOW DOES ME BEING MY SELF AFFECT ME?

You will feel more present and as such will find it easier to interact with others through the power of your truth. When you know your Self then you feel confident about what you do and how you interact with others. You will also be true to your work and those who are interacting with you in your workplace. They will feel your sincerity and openness towards the qualities of unconditional sharing and giving.

- Trust your Self. Have you ever felt the heart-warming feeling that comes when you trust your Self? Then you know what it is that you are looking for. Trust is built by your higher thoughts telling your logic that this is the way; it is safe to trust in the Self. In this way you are gradually transforming any doubts or fears that are present. See chapter "*I trust*".

- Listen to your intuitive heart logic. When you follow your inner compass through listening to your heart, then you will be able to transform your Ego - which holds and uses fear, expectation, need, desire and doubt - to control your logical perception of life. Self has no identity. It simply "is". See chapter "*I follow my inner compass*".

- Stay present and accept. When you are present then you can accept what is happening. When you accept what is happening then you will touch the true Self, your love and light, joy and peace. See chapters "*I am present*" and "*I accept.*"

THOUGHTS

A thought is an energy that is created by the mind. It is a force that has enormous potential because it is of universal consciousness. A thought is a "form" of energy that is the builder of society itself. It is the creative force of life and intentions. There are basically two levels of thought, the logical (third dimensional consciousness) and the higher mind (fourth dimensional consciousness). The following is a deeper insight into their meaning.

THOUGHTS AND LOGIC

This is our third dimensional consciousness. This level of consciousness is found in the left hemisphere of the brain. This consciousness is based on logical reasoning, a meaning that is physical in its outlook. Logic views the world through physical eyes. The consciousness of logic predominantly works around physical phenomena such as physical light, duality, the five physical senses, and emotions. Logic resonates with the laws of time, distance and matter. When using logic, it is difficult to reason with anything that does not fit into the physical world. The logical-minded person fears anything that cannot be seen or understood. He might for example justify paranormal happenings by saying they do not exist or that it is imagination playing tricks. This mindset has its limitations. It is mainly because logic is limited to its own level of consciousness, and as such does not have the capacity to expand beyond that level. The logic is important to help ground your higher consciousness in order to create a balanced physical and spiritual world. A stable logic is essential for spiritual development; otherwise the higher consciousness will not be able to bring the message of love to you.

Much of the logical reasoning and thoughts has taken humanity to where it is today. The sciences that are based on logical reasoning and fact-finding play an important role in all cultures. Medicine, physiology and psychology seek the meaning of life, and are working to find ways to improve the quality of life. There are however limitations in the scientific understanding of the human body. Two important bodies of energy are seldom recognised by the sciences. Those are the energies of the Spirit and the Soul. Each and every one of us has a Spirit and Soul. They are the creative forces that have built the physical body. The body is the end result of these two higher vibrations of consciousness. However, even today, there is an air of denial regarding these two phenomena. This is because when you talk about the Spirit and the Soul, it makes the logical brain stop. Logic cannot understand how spirit can communicate with it through telepathic means. It may understand theoretically, but few in these sciences experience it or train their minds to do so. To be intuitive means that you are overriding the logic to believe in something that has not yet appeared or happened, and that is mind-stopping. By being intuitive you are being spiritual.

THOUGHTS AND HIGHER MIND

Thought patterns in relation to the higher mind are not related to physical laws as the logic is. The right hemisphere of the brain holds your intuitive qualities of higher mind, which is fourth dimensional thinking. Logic and intuitive thoughts will complement each other as long as fear and judgement are not present. Then your choices become decisions instead. Decisions are taken from a holistic, non-judgemental, egoless point of view of the world. That is the difference between choosing (logic) and deciding (holistic).

ABOUT EMOTIONS OVERRIDING THE MIND

Some let their emotions flood their mind, which may show as forms of fanaticisms, frustrated idealisms and a feeling of being lost. It is interesting to note that this energy is not from the mind, it is from emotion. It is instead the result of emotional energy rising up into the mind to flood it. The mind itself and the original thought is pure, but when you let your emotions rise into the mind, then it becomes clouded. It is the same whenever you think negatively. It is what we do with our thoughts that create difficulties. If you allow your emotions to take over your rational thinking then you become lost. You can also become irrational due to the pressure that the emotions place on the mind.

Let us look at an example. Jealousy is a deep-seated emotional imbalance that is very destructive in its nature. When a person becomes extremely jealous of a partner, then their imagination begins to divert from their normal rational thinking. This can have a negative effect on their physical senses, such as the eyes. The jealous person may see you walking down a street with a friend, but will interpret it differently. It is wise to remember here that it is not the eyes themselves that tell the brain what to see, it is the other way around. It is the brain that interprets what the eyes see. Strong jealousy will overpower the mind by overriding the rational view. In other words, the jealous mind will imagine what is not there. The power of jealousy can even overpower how you speak, as words of anger will come to justify the feelings of jealousy. The jealous person is deeply imbalanced in their emotional body due to a lack of trust in themselves. They constantly seek rewards and attention, even at the cost of another person. These conditions cannot be transformed by using logic. They require you to direct higher consciousness towards the way you view and feel about the world. Below are three ways in which the emotional energy can affect your thinking. The examples are given to demonstrate why it is important to direct your thoughts through higher consciousness.

- You are overactive.

  If you are emotionally over-stimulated when working then that affects your mental condition. This can lead to furious activity or overworking, which is due to your determination to not be frustrated. It is here that physical will-power is used to make the plan work. This approach eventually results in the person breaking down as the nervous system cannot hold the stress. All of which can be avoided if the mental condition is changed and the correct rhythm on the physical plane is achieved.

- You are rebelling.

  The second condition is brought about by the state of rebellion which overshadows the life principle of peace. This very often brings about a violent emotional reaction, such as anger. The over-stimulation may be based upon the mental realisation of our responsibility to all things plus the recognition that your wishes are not materialising. But again the basic cause of the difficulties is emotional rebellion, and therefore it is not a mental condition. Bitterness, disgust, hatred and a sense of frustration can and do produce toxic conditions in the body. All of which can create a general poisoning of the physical body, which eventually brings about ill health. In such cases, the vision is often far bigger than the accomplishment, and this is what causes the emotional suffering. It is a condition to which you can become strongly attached as a means of confirmation, and often justification for the suffering. The Ego is present again. The cure can be found in one simple word: "Acceptance." This will lead to the avoidance of wasting time and energy by attempting the impossible. Acceptance takes you into being present, and when present you can use those moments to create the possible.

- Your body cannot cope with the demands.

Finally, there are difficulties caused by the failure of the physical body to measure up to the individuals' demands of life. Where this is the case there is normally nothing much that you can do. But when there is an eagerness to be creative then a great deal might be accomplished to bring about improvement. This will lay the foundation for a better function in another lifecycle. It is here that the continuing effort to perfect the physical body is also seeking its way forward during each lifetime. It is in human nature to go beyond the limitations that may be felt or experienced in any given lifespan and where the physical body feels that limited improvement will be sought, as long as your acceptance of life is lived from the heart.

TIME

WHAT IS THE MEANING OF TIME?

Time is given to us as a physical energy that helps to rule the logic and gives life structure. It is an elusive energy. Events come to us from the future into the present and end up as the past. A past that is irreversible. History is one such a measure of time. The human time clock is fixed to the movement of the Earth, making one rotation every 24 hours. This gives the time of days, weeks and months of the year, and places years into their various categories, such as decades and centuries. Nature also follows time but is conditioned by the seasons. When you look back at to how people interact with time, then it becomes more complicated. For simplicity reasons, time has been broken down into six categories that are connected to "Earth Laws". These physical laws clearly demonstrate how people interact with time and how it is built into our consciousness. The physical laws are time, distance and matter, past, present and future. Here is a summary of each aspect of time and how they impact upon our lives:

TIME: is measured by physical light speed. Physical light travels at exactly 299,792,458 meters per second. This is how the logical, left hemisphere of the brain, connects to light and assesses moving objects that travel within this light speed.

DISTANCE: the distance between Stockholm to London via airplane is measured by the speed of the aeroplane in connection to physical light speed. Measuring an object, such as a piece of wood, is carried out in imperial or metric. How long it takes you to drive from one location to another is measured in average speed according to time and distance. This gives you the time of arrival.

MATTER: is a denser form of quantum light, held together by electromagnetic forces and gravity. The physical body for example is created from light. Matter applies to all that you can physically see or touch; e.g. the earth and minerals, plants, animals and humans.

PAST: is a historical moment that you cannot change in any form. Everything that you have ever experienced is in the past, it has gone by. Your background, career, experiences, and activities are held in your past memories.

PRESENT: when you are being present you are living life fully because the past or future cannot influence you. The present moment is all we actually have, but many do not realise this fundamental law. Whenever you are present you are in your light, you shine. You are fully focused on what is occurring on all levels – mentally, emotionally and spiritual. You gain the full experience of life, moment to moment.

FUTURE: is an event or happening that has yet to materialise. It could be compared to a stock option. You buy something today to speculate about the future outcome of its value. This is an area of the unknown in which much effort is used to predict what the future holds. The entire stock market is based upon futuristic speculation. To try to predict the future is beyond logical reasoning. It creates stress because you are in great expectation. This drains the body of energy. If, however, you trust and accept what is to come rather than seeking to control or manipulate it, you will feel different about yourself and the world at large.

HOW DOES TIME AFFECT ME?

If you ask yourself this very basic question at any time of the day: "Where are my thoughts right now; are they in the past, present or future?" Your answer could be 60% in the past, 30% in the future and 10% in the present! Then ask yourself "why am I spending so much time and energy being in the past and in the future?" There could be many ways to justify why, but are they true? Or are there some hidden motives as to why you may spend so little time being present. We shall not go into these reasons, but instead focus on what it means to be present. Whenever you are not being present you are actually fighting time itself. You are either trying to catch up with it or you are trying to be ahead of it. Which strikes you as being the most influential in your lifestyle? This question creates a lot of stress because both are illusions of the logical mind, which are predominantly based on fear or expectations, and often both.

HOW DOES TIME AFFECT MY WORK?

If you are not self-employed, your work schedule may be fixed by your company, where you clock in and out of work. Your payment is often fixed to the amount of time you work. So you may clock in regularly, or if you are fortunate, you may have flexible hours that suit your life's routine. On the other hand you may be a project manager who has been given a set time to reach a certain goal, and the achievement of this also depends on another branch that may be in another country. There may be a timescale that you have committed yourself to. This may add to the pressure you already feel if, for example, the original timescale that you were given was optimistic. Whose responsibility is it to achieve the expected result within the timescale given? Here lies a fundamental point and a trap that many fall into. It could be that a number of events interfere with the set schedule. Has there been a reasonable allowance in the timescale of the project to cover any eventuality? If not then some strong pressure can be placed on certain people's shoulders. But why should it be like this? There can be a domino effect with many projects where the dominos are so closely aligned that there is no room for a small error. If you have to go home because of a strong cold, who is going to take over your responsibilities? Remember that the time clock does not stop for anyone. Are you the kind of person who carries on regardless of what is happening, even with a strong cold? If so who is in control, you or time itself? Or is it your higher Self who unconsciously may have given you the cold in order to take time off? It all depends on how you read the message.

HOW CAN I BALANCE MY TIME SHEET?

There is a natural rhythm to time which you can learn to embrace. It is called "trust." You certainly can never catch up with time. Through your acceptance of any given situation, you will automatically become present, in the moment. Then you will embrace the future because you know you can hold and manage whatever comes your way. This happens by you focusing on being present; it is a conscious effort that creates the reality for you.

If you look at your next assignment, ask yourself the basic question of whether it has been given enough time – including errors or lack of communication – to deal with the unforeseen? If you are able to set a respectable timescale, you may even finish before the deadline. Then everyone should be happy, shouldn't they. Will those above you choose to cut the expected time of the next scheduled project because you were ahead of time with the last one? This is often a trap that some fall into. There are always happenings, but how you deal with them is of importance in order to hold a positive flowing energy. This is an inner knowing you have which tells you that you can manage any situation that comes your way. And you can do that without losing your time and presence. By relaxing your thoughts about time, you may find that you will have time to do the necessary work and enjoy it. By not constantly looking at the clock, you are accepting and being present. Maybe not everything will be accomplished within the timeframe, but that which is important will be accomplished with greater joy.

THREE LEVELS OF CONSCIOUSNESS RISING

WHAT IS CONSCIOUSNESS RISING?

Different levels of consciousness rising have brought humans to where they are today. History demonstrates that human creativity is extremely diverse and increasingly innovative. One example of this is when fire was created by using wooden implements and flint stone. Or how weapons to hunt and kill evolved from the humble beginnings of the axe, the bow and arrow to the present day use of nuclear weapons. All of these required consciousness rising in order to develop the underlying innovative creativity within a person to discover and cross new frontiers. The many sciences demonstrate that the human mind is continuing to evolve to where it currently stands today.

The diagram to the right demonstrates in a simplistic way how human consciousness has, and still is evolving. The journey begins from the root race of humanity to the present day "ground floor" thinking that is evolving towards higher consciousness. There are two levels of consciousness that are connected to the cellar, which give a valuable insight into how the consciousness may be influential to your everyday living.

+2

+1

Ground Floor

- 1

- 2

Reference

LEVEL -2

This is the primal level of consciousness which has two main purposes. The first is that it grounds the physical body by helping you to be present within yourself, and not lost in the past or future. Secondly it holds the consciousness of survival and this is the oldest and deepest instinct you have. You want to survive in order to live, and you will often fight to preserve yourself from any harm or danger. There are many examples in human experience where the logic has been overridden by the need to survive, even at the cost of another person's life.

LEVEL -1

Sexual reproduction is a prime motivating factor here, in order to produce offspring that would hunt and gather as well as offer protection from other tribes. Very early on in this era, choice was awakened within the minds of the people. This created dualities that deepened reasoning that then began to expand the consciousness of the human mind to its present state. Choice helped to carry the expanding consciousness beyond pure survival and sexual needs, up into the third dimensional consciousness.

"GROUND FLOOR" THE THIRD DIMENSIONAL THINKING – LOGIC

This is the base level of consciousness today, where the majority of thought is presently being focused and used. Logical thoughts work through physical laws. These laws are time, distance and matter, past, present and future. They hold together the physical dimension that is chiefly responsible for the world we live in today. Logical thought is often referred to as box thinking. This term describes the consciousness of logic to be limited, or in the box. It is limited to its own particular understanding of physical laws, through which a logically-based person finds it difficult to embrace Universal laws. This level of consciousness has limited understanding of worldly events from a higher mind principle; this is due to the consciousness of the left hemisphere of the brain being logical. The logical reasoning is of great importance. The person with ability to reason without interference from emotions is a balanced logical thinker. This can lead to insight through balanced reasoning that is grounded by factual proof. Logic is becoming "old consciousness." There is a great shift in consciousness rising taking place right now on a global level. Days, weeks and months seems to be flying by, it is as if time itself is being condensed. A logically-based person tends to use judgement a lot. "Judgement" has been chosen as a word to demonstrate the meaning of "old consciousness." Judgement is pure Ego and it seeks to separate one from the other, which is why duality is closely connected to judgement. Whenever you say "I don't like this, I like that, I am better than you or I don't like that person because…" This is the Ego using judgement to justify itself. The Ego justifies itself in this way because it wants recognition, even at the cost of another person. Judgement is not a Universal law. It was created by the Ego which uses the logic to demonstrate its power. That power continually seeks to control your feelings and thoughts about everything that you interact with, consciously and unconsciously. An example of this is how humans continue to kill each other by passing judgement. Another aspect of lower consciousness – logic – is that it can only work at the ground floor level of thought, that of the third dimension. If you try to understand anything that is beyond logic, it will give you a headache. An example could be if you experience a supernatural happening, such as seeing a ghost. Or you could be trying to understand how your intuition works? This is why, when the mind cannot understand something, it will take you into fears that are linked to your past experiences or fears that are caused by you speculating about the future to try to justify your choices. You may continue to go round and round and get trapped in your own thoughts, and from here there is often no escape, unless you decide to work with yourself from a higher level of consciousness.

LEVEL +1; HIGHER CONSCIOUSNESS - FOURTH DIMENSION

When your consciousness is present on this level the consciousness cannot be corrupted by your lower nature, such as the Ego and third dimensional thinking. Higher consciousness holds the keys to liberating the Self to become a loving being, to be non-judgmental and present without fear. It holds key values such as trust and intuition which can give valuable insight into life itself. When your consciousness is moving up from the ground floor level you are beginning to examine what you see more deeply, and with different eyes. You may begin to ask questions about yourself, and one of these questions could be what motivates you in life. You may question your motives or become less judgemental and more accepting instead. Or you may begin to look at your fear issues in order to transform them into trust and faith. Whenever you are present on this level your tools are to accept, to love all things, to trust the Self, to become more intuitive and innovative, to not judge another or the Self, and learn the deeper meaning of being present. These are some of the key principles that you will study and experience while learning to hold the vibration of higher mind. This is in an effort to create a true blending of the third and fourth dimensional consciousnesses, which is required to lead a harmonious, balanced life. When the logic and the intuition are brought into balance they will complement each other towards viewing any given situation with a holistic outer perception and an inner knowing of what is true. When you are able to combine these two qualities, you use your full potential. Meditation is one way of learning how to integrate your logic and intuition.

LEVEL +2; HIGHER CONSCIOUSNESS - FIFTH DIMENSION

When you are fully aware of all life issues and are not lost in the lower nature, then you are being present in your fifth dimensional consciousness. You are love and light. You have peace of mind and heart. You shine with joy and have faith in all that you do. This is the level of higher mind awakening or enlightenment. When you have developed your consciousness to this point, you are walking your talk and living your truth. You are truly doing whilst being. All forms of lower consciousness such as Ego, logic, fears, expectations, needs, desires and restlessness no longer have a grip on your life. You will have transformed their lower negative vibrations from within yourself into ones of peace and acceptance. Your thoughts will be ones of loving care for others. Others may judge or even be angry with you, but their resentments will not affect you. When you have gained a deeper understanding of life, those experiences will carry your higher-minded insights and will assist you to serve from a deep, neutral loving place from within your heart. The qualities of such a person are often clear to see, because they are love, light, joy and peace. They shine!

WHAT IS STRESS?

Stress is about vibration. Every thought and feeling you have holds a certain vibration and is an energy force that must go somewhere, as all energies do. Stress is witnessed, felt and created in a variety of ways in society globally. It can be individual or group orientated. Stress arises through two main routes, the emotional aspect and the mental body (lower mind), and often both simultaneously. See also chapter *"Stress"* in the Fear and Control section. Both routes have a definite negative effect upon the central nervous system. Stress is strongly connected to the logic. Logic is consciousness ruled by time, distance and matter. These are earth-bound and are, in spiritual terms, called the third dimensional consciousness or 3D. Within these three (time, distance and matter) are held the concepts of past, present and future. These are the six main energy forms that help create our social structure, but at the same time are responsible for creating a large amount of stress, due to the incorrect use and understanding of their meaning and purpose. Let us have a look at how each of the six energy forms can create stress.

TIME

The time aspect is probably the most influential of all stress factors. This is because it cannot be controlled. You can never catch up with, or hold time. If you were able to then you would still be with the dinosaurs! Time holds the aspects of past, present and future. These aspects exist to help give humanity a deeper understanding of how time is constructed. Time gives us a structure to follow, like hours of the day, and months of the year. There are several formats for the measurement of time. For example, linear time and Mayan calendar time.

DISTANCE

Distance has at least two forms; the first being measured as inches, centimeters, miles or kilometers. The second aspect of measuring distance is through light speed, as in "light years away." These forms of measurement provide a means of measuring how long it will take to travel from A to B at a certain speed - be it in a car, train or spaceship.

MATTER

The material aspect of life is what is important here. How one thing is transformed, or made into another material. An example could be that iron ore is extracted from the ground and then melted into iron. This form of energy exchange created the industrial revolution that transformed the way we live, especially over the last two centuries. Humans are very materialistic in today's societies. The world's resources, such as the heavy metals of iron, copper and lead are being depleted, because more than needed is being consumed. Much stress arises from the need for more material things, which in turn puts stress on the world's resources. The world is over consumed and people are still not happy and content with life as it is. The need for material things has become a surrogate mother/father for many.

PAST

Memories and previous experiences have a strong bearing on how you relate to the past. What you create and why and how you create it can be highly impacted by past memories and experiences, especially if you are attached to them. This is also a seedbed for expectations and needs. Many lack presence and are often lost in their past, by continually reliving their past through their thoughts. This is where fears come from, and fear is a big creator of stress.

PRESENT

Stop your mind for a moment and consider that there is actually only one moment in your life, and that is the moment that you are in now. Everything else is an illusion of our imagination's creativity. Why is it that a gift is called "present?" It is because when you buy a gift for another person, you give it to that person with love in that moment, the *pre-sent* moment. The vibration of love can only be felt when fully present. This is because true love carries a vibration that is higher than the 3D consciousness, the earth-bound vibration. Love is a fourth dimensional vibration. It is free from the Ego or emotional influences. It is in fact purity of light. By learning to stay present you will experience another reality, the one of total freedom, peace and joy.

FUTURE

Fear of the future and the unknown are major causes of stress. If you do not trust yourself then you may want to know or seek to control what the future will bring. You speculate on what may come, you may also view pictures in your mind's eye of how you see the future and thus create expectations.

Many people are living either in the past or in the future and are very seldom present. Let us say that you are living your life 65% of the time in the past, thinking about things that have happened; and 20% in the future, thinking about things that you fear might happen or that you want to happen. That would leave you with 15% of your time being present. Playing with children is a great way of being present. Most of our society is built on the logical understanding of past and future, which is largely responsible for the stress factors that are being witnessed in western cultures and beyond. One example of this is the entire stock market, which is built upon futuristic analysis. Another example is the insurance industry which evaluates through past events the related probabilities of future unwanted events. People working in these fields must experience a great deal of stress simply because they are seldom present in their psyche due to their work being related to either the future or the past.

WHAT CREATES STRESS?

- Stress is created by negative feelings.

- Stress can be control related, such as targets which have to be reached.

- Stress is undoubtedly related to the factors of time, distance and matter.

- Stress can be passed on to you by others, often unknowingly.

WHAT BLOCKS ARE CREATED BY STRESS?

- Stress takes you away from being present.

- Stress will prevent you from seeing and feeling clearly.

- Stress leads people into places where they should not be (anger is one such place).

- Stress can be used as a weapon to keep people busy (to make someone feel guilty or to give them fear).

HOW CAN I UNDERSTAND MORE ABOUT MY STRESS?

Here are some aspects to study to help you understand more about stress.

STUDY HOW VARIOUS ENERGY FORMS WORK WITHIN AND AROUND THE PHYSICAL BODY.

How do you use your life force? Do you use your *physical will* or do you use your *spiritual will?* It is important to note that the spiritual force within the physical body is the prime motivator of the physical movements that you experience. It is directed by the soul, your higher consciousness. Your higher consciousness determines how strongly the spiritual will comes through. This also indicates how strong your life force is, the power of your inner light. THE PHYSICAL WILL: the physical will is based upon the male aspect of your psyche. The male aspect represents the power used to manifest your wishes or desires. The Ego can be very strong in this area as it drives to make things happen. It can override logic and the effects are the same for both men and women. The Ego's driving force is behind much of what is achieved on a material level. The physical will to do and achieve takes energy out of the body; it is a bit like draining your batteries. The

Ego's will to continually manifest your wishes or dreams can become a compelling energy that sometimes turns out to be destructive, either to the one using their willpower or to those in the line of fire. Much physical force is used in this way. The power of this force is however limited to the physical and mental abilities of the individual. It is inevitable that if you do not listen to your body then a crash of some kind will occur. This can be, for example, increased stress that leads to burnout! THE SPIRITUAL WILL: this is the opposite of the physical will. The spiritual will is female in its outlook upon life. The feminine represents the creative aspects of your psyche. The spiritual will is more intuitive and as such listens more deeply to what it feels; and acts accordingly. The spiritual willpower is a force that is manifested from your higher consciousness. It continually seeks to serve through the creative qualities and not primarily to make things happen. The spiritual will takes no energy out of the physical self. In fact it feeds it, giving it more vitality. You do not get burned out when you are in touch with the higher force of your spiritual will. You know when you are working with this energy. There is a certain kind of flow and it seems effortless. This energy usually follows the path of least resistance. It is a kind of channelling method. You are receiving from a higher source. The interesting thing about this is that you do not have to be spiritually minded to access this energy form. The only thing that is required is that you are true to your inner feelings of what you feel is right. You will intuitively know what, how and when to do something next for the greater good. POWER: the word "power" can be attributed to many things, as is mentioned above (physical and spiritual willpower). The source of divine power is a peaceful means of using the life force to be creative. Power is also related to many forms of energy, the power of thought for example. Thought is the energy that connects our different levels of consciousness and this is the first and most fundamental aspect to understand. The opening created by the thought helps to direct the energy in motion. This is a fact that has profound meaning for every human being on Earth.

STUDY VARIOUS WAYS TO RELAX AND CENTRE YOURSELF.

It is important to become less stressed. The techniques that you may want to study here are meditation and various breathing techniques. You can also study your attitudes and intentions in life, both with regards to yourself, and how you relate to others. DETACHMENT: indirectly this word does not mean separation; it means that you can take a step back from any given situation, for a moment or longer. This gives you an opportunity to observe what is happening from a neutral point of view. It is here that we are often tested to trust. To step back from a situation can be confronting, challenging and even seem to be disruptive, but beyond all forms of attachment and their emotional needs lay an inner knowing and peace. By detaching yourself from a situation there often comes greater awareness of what is occurring because you are not directly involved. True detachment liberates you from your Ego and emotional needs. These have been controlling your life force and have kept you from being in your power.

STUDY HOW YOU USE YOUR THOUGHTS IN EVERYDAY LIFE.

How you use your thoughts will either bring harmony or disharmony to your life. Your thoughts are projected through your words. The spoken word is a powerful form of communication that has been evolving for thousands of years. The words you use will be different if you are guided by your higher willpower than if you are being guided by your lower willpower. Right thinking will enable you to live in your truth, wrong and negative thinking will create a lot of stress. NON-CRITICAL: when you are non-critical in the way you express yourself, then you are non-judgemental. By studying how you can become non-judgemental will help you to get rid of your mind's conditioning of negative thoughts. Study how your Ego end emotions control your path by blocking your truth and liberty. THE EGO: this relates to your identity and the nature of your lower personality (emotions, needs, fears and expectations to name a few things that make up the lower personality). The Ego always seeks to be busy by achieving, and as such can use a lot of the body's energy to fulfil its needs. The Ego creates separation through judgement as a means of identity. It will judge all things as a means to separate you from your true Self. It seeks to keep you focused in the past and the future, or both at the same time as it tries to prevent you from being present. Your Ego creates stress in your life. See also chapter *"The Ego."* EMO-TIONS: your emotions are intertwined with the Ego. They are often difficult to separate. At times they can become one and the same. To a large degree, they control the lower mind. This is because the Ego's vibration is lower-consciousness orientated, and it only views the world as being black or white, right or wrong. Judgement is an example of how the Ego justifies its presence by separating people. Judgement is not truth. It is based upon self-belief patterns, conditionings and preferences (I don't like this, I like that). These aspects of the lower nature seek to control and hold the mind and body in shadow and prevent you from loving. Strong emotions can lead to great deal of stress if not managed correctly. TRUTH AND LIBERTY: these are fine qualities to aspire to. You cannot alter or change truth. Truth is light, there are no shadows and nothing can be hidden where there is light. It is the great liberator of life. Whenever you are present you are more deeply connected to the light because you are not living in the past or the future. The past and future are the domains of the Ego. The Ego avoids being held in the present at all costs because when you are present, the Ego cannot use fear to control you. The Ego wants to keep you in your dramas and for you to be the victim. In this manner the battle is raging between the lower and higher consciousnesses. SINGLE MINDED: when you are completely focused on something then you are being single minded. Sometimes when you are focused in this manner you are criticised for being self-ish, because you put everything aside to care for what you have taken interest in. But are you really being selfish? Have you felt guilty because of this? Being single minded is not a fault in itself, as long as the Ego is not present and you care for your true Self in what you are doing. INTENTIONS: There is an intention behind everything that you do. It may not be obvious, but your intention is connected to your feelings. If you wish to achieve something that is driven by your Ego or your emotions, then single mindedness can be negative. But when your feelings are clear of desires from the lower nature then your intentions are also clear to serve. Single mindedness in this aspect will then have a different meaning and purpose. You will most likely help others as a form of service. It can be, symbolically speaking, an arrow that is heading straight for its target, pushing everything else aside. If you are strong in your wishes and you are compassionate in your consideration for others, then it is a fine quality. Being focused can take you along a path that holds a great sense of peace, as long as it is not Ego-based.

WHAT IS SERVICE?

Service is brought about when your mind, body, spirit and soul seek to help others. Service is not a quality or a performance that must be achieved at all costs. It is not an activity which people must do. It is not a way to save the world, but it will help the world become better. This distinction must be clearly grasped and understood. Service is to care for others with no needs attached. It is an expression of the soul. All human beings are souls of instinct; therefore you have an inborn instinct that is individual to you. To be of service is the outstanding urge of the soul. To serve can also be a desire for a whole group of people. Neither theory nor aspiration can make you a real server. It is a quality that is found within all people who seek to help and touch others. Today we spend much of our time running after service, with an idea and effort to do good for others. You must be aware that often this service is not from the heart, but deeply covered by the personality of the Ego, which needs recognition and feedback for delivering the service. This can cause a lot of harm. The person who delivers service under these circumstances tries to impose their ideas of service and their personal techniques upon others. These people may have become sensitive to impression, but they often misinterpret the truth and are biased towards their personal needs. You must learn to lay the emphasis on soul contact and not on the Ego's side of service. If you take great care over how you serve then you will have greater soul contact with everyone. The service that is given will flow with spontaneity along the right line because the right rhythm is in place. The intent is from the soul and heart. This way will bear much fruit. Through this form of selfless service there will be a deeper flow of your spiritual life force. It is not the thought of what you should do that matters; it is simply what you do.

There is much theory about service and its expression, but sometimes it is a lot of talk and very little action. You may also fail to serve because you do not comprehend the meaning of why you are doing certain tasks. For example, the production of ethanol using corn is now causing food shortages, because the impulse to create a cleaner, cheaper fuel was far greater than the ability to see the situation from a holistic point of view. In this case the door was shut to real comprehension of the whole situation. The mind element was too active. You hold an underlying force that will eventually lead you towards helping others with a clear insight of what you have to offer in the form of true service. It is at times difficult to understand the strength of this urge but it can be enhanced with true morals and ethics. People's hearts are sound, but often asleep. Because of this, philosophy and religious theory have taken forms that often dictate rather than lead. To inspire and heal has often been presented in ways of obedience to masters and leaders. It is a matter of firstly listening to the service and obedience of your soul's calling that is required. In time you will be free from the holding of the Ego. It will lead you into your heart, which is the sign of one who is on their path to true service and spiritual liberation. Every person has special qualities. These inborn instincts are inseparable from your characteristics and hold certain qualities, which include the following:

• The power to contact and appreciate the world of meaning.

• The power of Love and to go out to meet others without fear. It is from here that selflessness is born.

- The capacity to grasp and to intuit ideas. This will give birth to the Spiritual will that is Egoless and selfless.

- The capacity to sense the unknown. This is a mystical quality that everyone has.

When fully understood and practiced, these points will lead you to becoming more open to life and the opportunities that are present. You will be serving selflessly.

Reference

Worry and Irritation

Let us discuss some of the most common of all causes of trouble and disease: worry and irritation. These factors have become more common in today's societies. Here are some of the reasons why:

- The world situation is such that the problems of uncertainty are touching everyone.

- The intercommunication between people has greatly increased due to the fact that people live in larger groups, such as big cities. It is inevitable that we produce an effect upon each other as never seen before. If one member of a group suffers, all members suffer.

- The increasing sensitivity to feelings has also become such that men and women are more in tune with each other's emotional conditions. The effect is that mental attitudes are more powerful. A person's growing concerns and worries are added to those of their colleagues, friends, children and everyone that they share a part of their lives with.

- People are to a greater degree taking on difficulties that belong to someone else. This can happen telepathically and subconsciously, and can also carry an element of foresight as more people develop their psychic abilities.

- The age of instant information via the media connects people globally in seconds.

These areas give us an insight into to how difficult it is for people to interact in general. The problems that arise out of energies like worry and irritation must be harmonised to prevent stress.

WHY ARE THE DIFFICULTIES OF THE EMOTIONAL BODY SO SERIOUS?

Worry and irritation are stored as negative energies in the emotional body. See chapter *"The Emotional Body."* Worry and irritation are dangerous because:

- They lower the vitality of a person to a point where they become prone to illness.

- The individual that is highly infected by the influences of the emotional body finds it increasingly difficult to breathe freely. Asthma is one such condition.

- The conditions of fear, worry and irritation are so widespread today; it might be regarded as epidemic.

- Irritation (not worry) is inflammatory in its effects. You can for example lose your temper more easily because there is an underlying stress that must surface. Such inflammation is sometimes hard to bear, which often leads to great difficulties. It is interesting to note that certain eye conditions are caused this way.

- Worry and irritation prevent true vision, they shut out the view. The person who holds these conditions sees nothing but the cause of their complaints, which can lead to the victim syndrome, the selfish I. See also chapter *"The Ego."* You can become so lost in self-pity, self-consideration, or in a focused negative condition that your vision is narrowed, and the life is hindered. It may also limit the life of the people that you are connected to.

Some illnesses are due to the effects of worry and irritation. They also cause discomfort, such as restlessness. Any worry or irritation that is held in the emotional body may turn into a violent activity whenever a person is put under stress. When this occurs, tempers may rise and you will feel the anger. This is a mirror effect that is often the end result of stress. See chapter *"The Mirror effect."* Intense worry or prolonged irritation pours like a stream of emotional energy into the solar plexus centre because this is the natural place for it to go. This often strengthens that centre into a condition of intense disturbance that affects the whole abdominal area, such as the stomach, pancreas, gall duct and bladder. Due to this fact, those who are caught and affected by emotional imbalance in this manner may show signs of indigestion or gastric conditions in connection to the gall bladder.

The above information shows that worry and irritation come in many forms, and for a variety of reasons. If worry and irritation are permitted to continue, then greater difficulties can arise. One such difficulty is that emotional stimulation can rise into the mental body and develop into fear, which is a factor that can have a real hold on a person's life. Worry can override all rational and intuitive behaviour. It can create a state of confusion that can develop into a state of distrusting yourself and others around you. This is largely due to the nervous centre breaking down from the vibration of negative thoughts. This can lead to the body becoming less stable as all energy is being directed to the head in an effort to work things out. A person who worries a lot should practice being present to still their mind. See chapter *"Worry"* for help on how to transform worries and irritation.

All forms of worry create irritation. Generally speaking, this is felt as a distinct lack of trust that needs to be balanced. The irritation is expansive because it is related to the build-up of the pressures that your frustrations lay down in your psyche. These mainly arise out of such factors as expectations not being met. This can prevent you from taking decisive positive actions and moving forward. All forms of energy seek truth. If you have worries and you have no way of dealing with them, then you are in danger of locking them in. They will then either be held in your emotional body or in your consciousness. When this occurs, the central nervous system becomes devitalised which produces a negative effect on the spleen, kidneys and gall bladder. The results are felt as a general loss of vitality in the physical body. Worry is a bit like the baggage we carry around with us on our journeys. We tend to say "we are going that way anyway, so why take it along too?" Worry also relates deeply to not trusting the higher Self and your intuitive aspect. Some refer to this to the Universal flow of life. When you lack trust, you protect or overprotect yourself or others. So learn to trust and your worries will over time be transformed. See chapter *"I trust"* and *"The Self."*

Welcome to the light way!

As more and more people transform their fears and the need for control diminishes, then great things will happen. Not only will you as an individual have a true sense of awareness and a loving presence of joy and peace, you will also contribute to a long-awaited transformation to a higher level of consciousness. By transforming your fears you will have greater access to your intuition and you will be more present in the light. You will positively touch others in your environment through your consciousness rising. Your contribution in this manner is very important, and the more people who do this inner-work, the faster the transformation will become. Your relationships at home will change. The work environment will be lighter. New ways to do business will emerge. Whole societies will change as people stand strong in their trust.

We welcome you to experience life and thank you for joining us!

making **messages** from
loving hearts
available to a **global** audience

cocreators @lightspira.com
www.lightspira.com

Lightning Source UK Ltd.
Milton Keynes UK
UKOW06f1227311017
311942UK00009B/166/P